Bentley, about 1930

From the painting by F. Gordon Crosby

FORTY YEARS
OF MOTORING

1919–1959

The Story of National Benzole

BY EDWARD YOUNG

STANLEY PAUL
London

STANLEY PAUL & CO. LTD

178–202 Great Portland Street, London, W.1

AN IMPRINT OF THE HUTCHINSON GROUP

London Melbourne Sydney
Auckland Bombay Toronto
Johannesburg New York

★

First published 1959

Designed and produced by Rainbird, McLean Ltd
Set in Baskerville type face and printed in Great
Britain by Taylor Garnett Evans & Co. Ltd
Watford, Hertfordshire

Author's Foreword

THIS book began as a modest history of a remarkably successful British commercial enterprise, the National Benzole Company. As the work proceeded, however, it began to touch on so many points in the development of the motor car itself that by gradual stages, and almost before I was aware of it, I found myself embarked on a brief survey of motoring during those same forty years from 1919 to 1959.

It has been written for the ordinary "man in the street"—perhaps "man on the road" would be an apter expression—rather than for the expert. In such a rapid account of a period so rich in technical ingenuity and progress it is inevitable that much has had to be left out. The expert will no doubt find exceptions to disprove some of my generalizations, though I hope he will not be able to fault me on my facts. The facts have been checked against a wide variety of sources, records and publications too numerous to list in their entirety, though I should like to mention especially those excellent books *The Vintage Motor Car* by Cecil Clutton and John Stanford, *Motoring Entente* by Ian Nickols and Kent Karslake, *The Sports Car* by John Stanford, *British Sports Cars* by Gregor Grant and *The Racing Car* by Cecil Clutton, Cyril Posthumus and Denis Jenkinson.

The illustrations have come from the owners of Vintage cars, from photographic libraries and agencies, from motor manufacturers and many others, all of whom are gratefully acknowledged on page 9. Special thanks are, however, due to the Curator of the Montagu Motor Museum at

5

Beaulieu and to the Secretary of the Bentley Drivers Club for their kindness in putting me in touch with the owners of many cars, and also to Mrs Janey O'Riordan for her indefatigable assistance in hunting down the illustrations I needed.

Finally, but above all, I have to thank my friend Aubrey Forshaw for his uncomplaining patience in checking through the manuscript and the proofs and for saving me from making too many wild statements, erroneous judgments and positive howlers.

E. Y.

Contents

ACKNOWLEDGMENTS

Thanks are due to the following for permission to use the photographs on the pages indicated:

A. C. Cars Ltd., 158 (*upper*)
Aston Martin Lagonda Ltd., 93, 122, 163
Austin Motor Co. Ltd., 152 (*lower*), 154 (*lower*)
The Autocar, colour frontispiece, 46, colour plate facing 73, 74, 75
Patrick Benjafield, 116
Bristol Siddeley Engines Ltd., 158 (*lower*)
Messrs. William Butler & Co., 34
Citroen Cars Ltd., 149 (*upper*)
The Cooper Car Co. Ltd., 170
Elliott & Fry, Ltd., 27
Fayer, 36
Fox photos Ltd., 20, 64, 76, 85, 86, 87, 114, 119, 127, 129 (*upper*),
    168, 172 (*lower*)
John R. Freeman & Co., colour frontispiece, colour plate facing 73
A. F. C. Hillstead, 71
Jaguar Cars Ltd., 123, 124, 156, 162
Jowett Engineering Ltd., 40
Keystone Press Agency, Ltd., 17, 31, 47, 50, 57, 118, 133, 157, colour
    plate facing 160, 160, 167, 169 (*upper*), 171, 173, 182
George H. Lanchester, 33
Lotus Engineering Co. Ltd., 169 (*lower*)
G. E. Milligen, 117
Mirrorpic, 108
The Montagu Motor Museum, 53 (*lower*), 62 (*upper*)
The Motor, 58 (*lower*), 73
The Nuffield Organization, 48, 111 (*lower*), 112 (*upper*), 145 (*lower*),
    152 (*upper*), 154 (*upper*)
Radio Times Hulton Picture Library, 12, 13, 14, 18 (*lower*), 29, 42,
    45, 51, 52, 54, 55, 58 (*upper*), 60 (*upper*), 63, 71 (*lower*), 89, 90, 92,
    111 (*upper*), 115, 126, 129 (*lower*), 140, 165, 172 (*upper*)
Renault Ltd., 149 (*lower*)
Rolls-Royce Ltd., 60 (*lower*), 112 (*lower*), 113, 150, 151
Rootes Motors Ltd., 77, 80, 81, 82, 84, 145 (*upper*), 146
John A. Rose, 174
The Rover Co. Ltd., 148
The Shell Petroleum Co. Ltd., 65
Derek Smith, 66, 69, 91
The Sport and General Press Agency Ltd., 23, 125, 164, 166
The Standard Motor Co. Ltd., 147
David Thirlby, 16, 94, 120, 121
The Trojan Owners Club, 49
Vauxhall Motors Ltd., 43, 153

9

CHAPTER I

Motoring in 1919

The comfortable motorist of today, with his air-tight saloon, his heater, his demister, his windscreen washers, his synchromesh or automatic gears, independent front suspension, finger-light steering – fitted radio, too, probably – will find it hard to remember (supposing he is old enough to do so) how far the "horseless carriage" has travelled since 1919, and what the conditions of ordinary motoring were like only forty years ago.

In those days to own a car at all was the exception rather than the rule, but if you had one it would probably be an open one, for (unlike today) saloons were a good deal more expensive. A car was largely a hand-made job, and saloon framework had to be made out of wood by a skilled coach-builder – and even then would usually develop irritating rattles in quite a short time. However, your open car would have a hood folded back behind the rear seats, ready to erect if it should come on to rain. Unfortunately there were no such things as windscreen wipers, and when it rained the top half of the screen had to be opened forward on a hinge so that you could see where you were going – just when you needed its protection most. Perhaps there really was less rain in those halcyon days – at any rate, inclement weather was something you accepted and wrapped up against and your lady passengers, enveloped in dust-coats, would keep their hats and their hair in place with veils tucked under their chins and survey the gently passing countryside from the elegant elevation of the comfortably upholstered rear seats. Some of the smarter touring cars had an additional windscreen to protect the back-seat passengers. If you were comfortably off you might have a landaulette, or "coupé de ville", with high coachwork to accommodate the tall headgear which both you and your wife were apt to wear at that time; but it would not occur to you to spare a thought for your unfortunate "man" exposed to the elements in the driving seat. Whatever your car its lines tended to be vertical rather than horizontal, and still bore traces of its horse-drawn ancestry.

The law required you, as it still does of course, to carry some means of giving audible warning of your approach. In 1919, unless you were the lucky owner of a "Silver Ghost", your car probably made enough noise to render such warning unnecessary, but your bulb horn or your Klaxon press-plunger startler provided a highly satisfactory means of expressing your opinion of a slow-footed pedestrian or an idiotic fellow-motorist. The modern electric horn or hooter, operated by a smart biff on the steering wheel, only came in with the general improvement of electrical equipment. It was not long, after all, since headlamps had been lit by acetylene. The electric starter, though pretty well established in America (it was already standard even on the current version of the Ford Model T), was by no means universal in Britain, and it was as well to have a strong right arm for winding on a cold morning – remembering to put the gear lever into neutral and keep your thumb *behind* the handle. (Nowadays the manufacturers tend to dispense with the handle altogether, a tendency not everyone will approve.)

Chauffeur-driven Daimler 45-h.p. landaulette of 1914

It was happening even then. This queue of cars waiting to get into Ascot in 1920 gives their drivers (see them leaning impatiently from their driving-seats) a foretaste of the traffic conditions to come. One party has decided to get out and walk the rest of the way. Watched by a rather warm-looking policeman Matilda looks both ways to make sure nothing is coming, while Alfred helps Gertrude to dismount, which she can do gracefully without showing too much leg, unlike her future grand-daughters. This charming photograph shows several typical cars of the period.

13

Piccadilly Circus in the early 1920's, looking towards Coventry Street. If you were a play-goer at that time you may be able to guess the exact year, for according to the No. 14 bus Irene Vanbrugh was playing the lead in *Eileen* at the Globe Theatre, and behind the figure of Eros it would appear that Harry Lauder was top of the bill at the Pavilion. This was in the days before the Circus became a round-about. Pedestrians could walk across the traffic with a reasonable chance of reaching the other side alive, and the old flower-sellers were still doing a thriving trade—a trade that was killed, alas, by later traffic conditions. On the other hand it is comforting to observe how many of the commercial advertisers are still going today; it evidently pays to advertise. Note the Tilling bus amongst the Generals, all open-topped, and the fact that bus route numbers have not changed even today. If you hailed a cab then it would probably be a De Dion Bouton.

Brakes operated on rear wheels only, but they were adequate enough for the comparatively low speeds then available to the ordinary motorist. The official speed limit, in fact, was still 20 m.p.h. – though this was a great advance on the early days when the law forbade the motorist to move without a man walking in front (a law whose repeal in 1896 is still celebrated by the annual Veteran Car Run from London to Brighton). Even the speed limit of 20, which remained in force until the Road Traffic Act of 1930, was perhaps no great hardship in the immediate post-war days, since the lack of shock-absorbers and the general state of road surfaces meant that speeds much in excess of 20 m.p.h. led to an uncomfortable passage for all concerned.

Bad weather might call for a certain stoicism, but good weather could bring its trials too. Nowadays in Britain un-"metalled" roads are fairly rare, but in 1919 on a dry summer's day you would be wise to wear protective goggles, for your passage along almost any high-way would be marked by a dust-cloud that would do credit to a buffalo stampede across the prairie. Water-cooling systems were less efficient than they are today, and on a hot afternoon you would be lucky if you got to the top of Porlock Hill without your radiator boiling over. But at least you could see it was happening: in the modern car, unless you keep a pretty constant eye on your water temperature gauge (if you have one), you can boil all your water away in blissful ignorance until your engine seizes up and lands you in for an expensive repair job.

Garages were few and far between, and they seemed fewer and farther if you happened to break down or run out of petrol. You would have to try to remedy the fault yourself, or wait for the next motorist who might happen along – other motorists would always stop and give you a hand in those days. You would carry a tool box and a couple of spare cans of petrol on your running-board. (Running-boards, remember? But why *running*-boards?)

If you wanted a fast car you would have to be fairly rich. Speed could only be achieved with comparatively large engines. If you were impecunious and young, and determined to be mobile at all costs, you might indulge in one of those abominable "cycle-cars" which enjoyed a brief popularity immediately after the 1914 war and were mercifully killed by the rapid advance of the light car in the early 'twenties. The cycle-car was little more than a somewhat unstable "bedstead" on wheels, often with a wooden chassis-frame and sides made of plywood or even wickerwork, the whole chain-driven or even belt-driven by a low-powered two-cylinder engine. There were one or two honourable exceptions, notably the G.N., forbear of the later Frazer Nash, but most of them were unreliable and positively suicidal to drive.

One of the "honourable exceptions", a 1920 G.N. cycle-car tourer, made by A. Frazer-Nash and H. R. Godfrey. The transmission principle, with a separate chain for each gear, was carried forward in the Frazer Nash cars well into the 'thirties. (See also illustration on page 120).

A pre-war version of the Ford Model T. Note the open sides, high seats, hood straps, narrow tyres, flat mudguards. As to coachwork, Ford said you could have any colour you wanted so long as it was black.

Many of the cars on the market bore names which are still with us today: Humber, Wolseley, Sunbeam, Rover, Morris, Austin and so on. The historic Ford Model T, which first appeared in America in 1908 and had been built in Manchester for the British market since 1910, was already becoming a familiar sight on our roads, especially in the country districts where its simplicity of maintenance, high clearance and general toughness made it an ideal working car. Vauxhalls, having made motoring history shortly before the war with their "Prince Henry" fast touring car, had now developed from it a

17

A British-manufactured Ford Model T of 1923. Though considerably modified from earlier versions, it was still unmistakably a "Tin Lizzy".

The man on the pavement has recognised the Royal Car. Here is King George the Fifth arriving at Ascot in his Daimler. The year is 1913, but Daimlers were so conservative that it might be any year in the early 'twenties.

The British challenge to the Model T, the popular bull-nose Morris Cowley.
First produced in 1919, it was soon put on to a mass-production basis and
became a familiar part of the English scene.

new sports car which was to become known as the "30/98" and set
the standard for the coming sports car boom of the 1920's. The name
of Daimler goes back to the very dawn of motoring, for though Carl
Benz was the first man to start manufacturing motor cars (in
1885), Gottlieb Daimler followed within a few months. The Daimler
car was introduced to England in 1890 by F. R. Simms, founder of
the R.A.C., and later manufactured here by the Daimler Motor
Syndicate. Our Royal Family travelled in Daimler cars from very
early on, and still patronise them today. Meanwhile the Hon. C. S.
Rolls and Henry Royce had already established the "Silver Ghost"
as "the best car in the world".

Facing: The one and only original Rolls-Royce "Silver Ghost", which is preserved today in pristine condition and still in good running order after completing nearly half a million miles. The "Silver Ghost", a 40/50 h.p. six-cylinder car, was first built in 1906 and had a phenomenal production run of nineteen years.

Below: A 1904 Peugeot being polished up in preparation for the London Cavalcade of Motoring held before King George the Sixth in 1946. The "Silver Ghost" opposite, though built only two years after this Peugeot, showed a considerable advance in design.

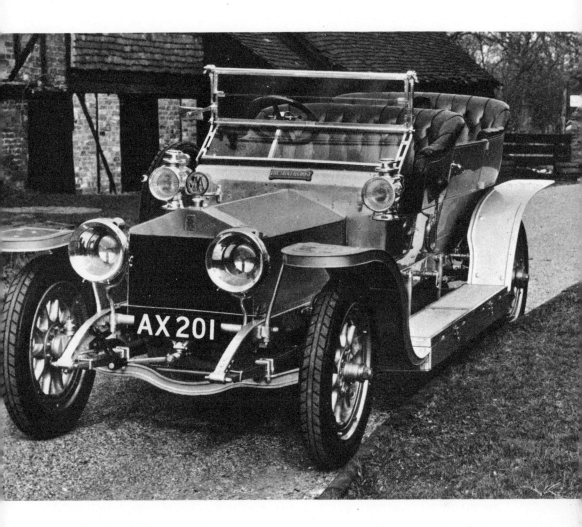

There is no doubt that motoring was by now accepted as something that had come to stay and form part of everyday life. The early hostility to the new-fangled monster was subsiding. The Automobile Club of Great Britain and Ireland, founded in 1897, had received Royal recognition and became the R.A.C. as long ago as 1907. The Automobile Association, founded in 1905, demonstrated the military capabilities of the motor car when in 1909, at the instigation of its Secretary, Sir Stenson Cooke, a fleet of members' cars transported a whole battalion of the Guards from London to Brighton. The war itself provided a severe testing-ground of the motor car

21

as such, and the undoubted success of the Rolls-Royce armoured cars and the Vauxhall, Crossley and Sunbeam staff cars (not to mention the new tanks) in all conditions of weather and terrain had emphasised the possibilities of mechanical transport and its general reliability.

King George the Fifth visits Vimy Ridge in a Vauxhall staff car

Reliability was not, however, a word you could apply to some of the petrol obtainable at this time, though you had to pay 3s. 6½d. a gallon for it – a stiff price for those days. There were none of the petrol-filling stations we take for granted – even petrol pumps did not exist as yet, though they were to appear very shortly (the first one to be erected in Britain was behind the Craven Arms Hotel in Shrewsbury). You got your petrol by pulling up at an untidy-looking garage workshop, and instead of sitting in your driving seat and being waited on by a white-coated attendant you probably had to go in and find a mechanic and persuade him to come out from under whatever he was mending and take time off to oblige you with a two-gallon can or two. You could also buy petrol from cycle agents, household ironmongers, village blacksmiths, and even from some inns and chemists. It was delivered to depots by rail, and thence to the retail outlets in cans, sometimes by open lorry but usually by horse and cart. The petrol you bought was often dirty, and on occasion water had an uncanny habit of finding its way into it.

But already an increasing number of motorists had cottoned on to the advantages of using a new fuel called benzole. They found that it gave better performance generally, made for easier starting, prevented engine-knock or "pinking", and gave more power, and therefore more miles, to the gallon. Enthusiasts liked to use it neat, but the trouble was to get enough of it. Benzole distribution was a haphazard business, and since neat benzole, with its more concentrated power, needed more air in the combustion mixture, and

An early photograph of Brooklands, but what is the occasion? A race?—yet the cars seem well burdened with passengers, and the course steward is getting in somebody's way. A parade?—but why all this overtaking? One car is being forced perilously near the inside edge.

therefore required an adjustment to the carburettor, the motorist got rather irritated if he found difficulty in obtaining supplies of it. So most benzole devotees bought it when they could and eked it out by adding it to the petrol in their tanks. The proportion of benzole to petrol was thus a somewhat casual affair, and led to considerable variety in performance. There was another snag too. Benzole is heavier than petrol; unless the two are scientifically blended the benzole will sink to the lower half of the tank, and the motorist of 1919 would therefore find performance gradually deteriorating as the benzole got used up first.

Nevertheless the demand for benzole was steadily increasing. What exactly was this new fuel which threatened to become a serious rival to petrol on the threshold of the age of popular motoring?

CHAPTER 2

The Discovery of Benzole

As you sit roasting your toes in front of a blazing coal fire on a foggy day in January, watching the smoke vanish up the chimney to add your quota to the smog outside, you may not realise that the smoke contains a percentage of motor spirit which would be more useful in the tank of your car. Your answer would be that you don't care, you *like* sitting in front of a live coal fire – and who shall blame you? Nevertheless the fact is there: every 1-cwt. bag of coal delivered to your home contains at least a pint of benzole.

You have probably noticed in that same fire in your grate occasional little spurts of ignited gas hissing out of the lumps of coal. Coal was mined and burnt for centuries before anyone thought of harnessing this gas in any way. Certainly no one did anything practical about it until 1792 when that remarkably versatile engineer Murdock (who incidentally built a working model of a steam road carriage some fifteen years before Trevithick produced his first successful machine) actually lit his home at Redruth with coal gas. It was not until twenty years later that coal gas was made on anything like a commercial scale. The first man who seriously tried to find out what coal is made of was G. T. Accum, who in the early 1800's obtained a number of products from it. In the History of Science Museum at Oxford is a collection of bottles containing samples of these materials, and one of the bottles, bearing the label "Highly Rectified Essential Oil", contains a liquid which looks like, smells like and is expertly considered to be – benzene. (Refined benzole, by the way, is 60 per cent benzene, plus toluene and xylene.)

Early in the nineteenth century an oil gas made from whale and

25

other oils was put on the market in portable cylinders. This gas, when being compressed for insertion into the cylinders, deposited a small residue of oil. The oil was analysed by Faraday, who in 1825 separated from it a liquid which he called bi-carburet of hydrogen; from the details he recorded it is clear that he had in fact isolated benzene in a fairly pure form. When testing it with nitric acid he noticed that it gave off an odour "exceedingly like that of almonds". Nowadays the name "aromatics" is given to the particular group of valuable power-producing hydrocarbons that go to make up benzole – benzene deriving from the sweet-smelling gum benzoin, toluene from tolu balsam, and xylene providing the characteristic aroma in wood naphtha.

Faraday also dropped a hint that the same liquid could probably be obtained from coal-gas, but it was to be some fifty years before the hint was followed up and found to be correct. Meanwhile, though several scientists had observed the presence of benzole in coal tar, in the first half of the nineteenth century there was no industrial requirement for it and therefore no incentive to anyone to extract it on a commercial scale.

The situation was changed in 1856 when Perkin discovered a way of making a synthetic mauve dye, in which benzole was an essential constituent, and so laid the foundation of the artificial dyestuff industry. From this discovery stemmed the whole of the later use of benzole in the manufacture of dyes, perfumes, drugs, antiseptics, explosives and so on. From 1856 onwards, therefore, there developed a steadily increasing demand for the aromatic hydrocarbons present in benzole, but until the turn of the century virtually the only commercial source of benzole was coal tar – a residue formed in the production of coal gas which had until then been regarded by the gas manufacturers as a positive nuisance!

A few years before Perkin's discovery, Mansfield had taken out a patent for distilling benzole from coal tar, but before he could develop it into practical form he was killed in a fire which broke out when he was preparing samples of benzene for the Paris Exhibition of 1855. However his work was carried on by Coupier, who constructed the first still of appreciable size and so put the production of benzole on a commercial basis. Meanwhile various experiments were being carried out in the extraction of benzole from coal gas, and in 1875 Young devised an apparatus which was in principle the same as that used today. Thus the way was opened up for benzole extraction to become a highly important component of two major British industries – the gas industry and the iron and steel industry, both of which turn coal into coke on a huge scale.

It was not until the early 1900's, however, that benzole began to be marketed as a rival motor fuel to petrol. And meanwhile petrol and benzole were by no means the only forms of power for vehicle propulsion that had been occupying the attentions of inventors in the evolution of the horseless carriage.

Sir W. H. Perkin, who at the age of eighteen accidentally discovered the dyeing properties of aniline while he was engaged in a vain attempt to make synthetic quinine.

CHAPTER 3

Getting Rid of the Horse

At the R.A.C. headquarters in Pall Mall can be seen a model of the first self-propelled vehicle ever built. It was made in 1770 by Captain Cugnot, a French artillery officer, with financial assistance from the French War Office. Driven by steam, it had a huge globe-shaped boiler overhanging in front in order to balance the weight of the field-gun which was to be mounted on the rear of the carriage. The whole thing proved too cumbersome ever to go into action, but it did move – literally – under its own steam, even though its top speed was three miles an hour. Unfortunately the vehicle took a Paris street corner too fast and overturned, and the unlucky inventor achieved the dubious honour of being the first motorist on record to be thrown into prison for dangerous driving.

Nevertheless steam was used as the motive power of the large number of horseless carriages built, especially in England, in the first half of the nineteenth century. Richard Trevithick led the way with his steam carriage of 1803, which set horses bolting and ladies fainting when it was first driven in the streets of London. Regular steam coach services were operated in various parts of the country, but the belligerent opposition of the horse-coach owners, prohibitive tolls on the turnpikes, constant mechanical troubles, the liability of boilers to burst and kill passengers, the rapid development of the railways, and finally the "Red Flag" Act of 1865, all proved too much for the steam carriage as a means of road transport, and for the rest of the century virtually no self-propelled road vehicles were built in England. It was left to Germany and France, unhampered by severely restrictive traffic laws, to continue the search for suitable

Contemporary print illustrating one of M. Cugnot's mishaps and the importance of efficient brakes and steering.

means of self-propulsion, and to Germany in particular to invent the first marketable petrol motor car.

Steam was seriously discredited by its poor showing in the historic motor race of 1895 from Paris to Bordeaux and back, in which steam vehicles were decisively defeated by the new petrol cars. Yet seven years later Serpollet set up a new speed record in his steam car by travelling at 75 m.p.h. over a kilometre, and though it was a petrol car which in 1904 first reached 100 m.p.h. it was Stanley's specially built steam car which covered a mile at 127 m.p.h. in Florida in the same year – a world speed record which remained undefeated for sixteen years! By this time steam cars were being fired by liquid fuel – petrol or paraffin – instead of coal or coke, but though they continued to be built for a few years yet, especially in America (where the White steam car, with its silent running and gearless flexibility, achieved great popularity for a time), it was becoming clear that their days were numbered.

Another smooth and silent self-propelled vehicle was the electric car, many examples of which were to be seen in the early years of this century, especially as a brougham for short-distance motoring in town society. But the heaviness of the batteries and the need for constant re-charging made the electric car useless for serious motoring.

Meanwhile, though petrol was used for the majority of the new internal combustion motor cars being designed and built in Germany and France in those early days, many inventors were experimenting with other fuels. Even moth balls were tried, as witness H. O. Duncan in his fascinating motoring miscellany *The World on Wheels*:

During some fuel tests in 1904, Chenier and Lion used an old Peugeot car to demonstrate the possibility of employing naphthaline or naphtha balls such as are sold by all oil merchants for preserving clothes from the attack of moths. These naphtha balls are a by-product of tar and have practically the same composition as paraffin. By melting them in a special apparatus fixed to the engine, the experimenters thought that they would get a very good result. The balls were placed in a box with a pipe heated by the exhaust communicating with the combustion chamber. The car ran with great regularity over a $37\frac{1}{4}$-mile course and consumed 13.2 pounds of naphtha balls. The only objection to this fuel was the intolerable smell of the exhaust. The cost of running the car was about one-half that of petrol.

One of the early experimental alternative fuels was alcohol. Great interest in this possibility was taken in the early years of this century, especially in France where over-production in the government-controlled sugar-beet industry in Picardy was causing a considerable economic crisis. It was hoped that the new automobile industry might absorb the surplus production of alcohol from sugar beet; alcohol car races were organised, directly encouraged by the French Ministry of Agriculture, and 1902 was actually designated "Alcohol Year". For various reasons, however, alcohol never came to the fore as a motor spirit. One reason was that as soon as there began to be a demand for it the price rose above that of petrol, another was its hygroscopic nature, and it is moreover not easy to "de-nature" it to render it unfit for drinking without at the same time reducing its value as a fuel.

It was benzole which was to cause most concern amongst the petrol companies.

Steam and electricity gave way before the advance of the internal combustion engine. The Germans were the first to make practicable motor cars on a commercial scale. Carl Benz made his first car in 1885, and Gottlieb Daimler was only a few months behind. Here, still going strong in the Veteran Car Run to Brighton in 1955, are an 1899 Benz (right) and a 1900 Daimler.

31

CHAPTER 4

The New Motor Fuel

Although the use of benzole was at first confined to dye-stuffs and a few other chemical industries, its value as a motor fuel was beginning to be recognised as far back as 1893. In that year Dr Fred Lanchester, a brilliant engineer who had been working on gas engines in Birmingham, designed a single-cylinder engine fuelled by benzole, put it into a boat and so produced the first motor-boat to be built in this country: it was a light-draught launch propelled by a stern paddle-wheel and enjoyed several years of useful life on the upper reaches of the Thames. In 1895 he built an experimental phaeton, with a single-cylinder 5 h.p. engine, which also ran on benzole and – in defiance of the "Red Flag" Act – was driven on the high roads at a comfortable cruising speed of 12 m.p.h. This vehicle was the first serious attempt at a full-size internal-combustion motor car produced in Great Britain, an individual design owing nothing to current Continental practice but evolved on original scientific lines. Next Lanchester built an 8 h.p. two-seater phaeton which went at 20–25 m.p.h. and was one of the cars to complete the course in the 1,000-mile Trial from London to Edinburgh and back organised by the Automobile Club in 1900. The first Lanchester car actually to go into market production was the 10 h.p. car launched in that year.

Slowly the idea of using benzole as a motor fuel began to gain ground in different parts of the country. In 1903 William Butler & Company of Bristol formed a subsidiary company to market benzole throughout the West of England, selling in two-gallon cans at a shilling a gallon and undercutting the petrol suppliers. About the same time in Staffordshire the Chatterley Coal and Iron Company were seeking ways to sell off some of their surplus by-product of

32

The first British-built, British-designed motor car, Dr. F. W. Lanchester's experimental phaeton of 1895. Like his earlier motor-boat, it ran on benzole.

benzole; in recent years a Mr Fred Daley has given us an account of the road tests he carried out on their behalf:

A 63-gallon cask was allowed me for a thorough test. I tested it under all conditions, hail, rain, snow, and occasionally sunshine, for it was February – and the year, unless my memory plays me false, was 1904. The car on which the test was made was a 16-20 h.p. Clement-Talbot, 1903 model. When I had completed the test my report was: Hill-climbing very much better than on petrol (more power on hills); consumption 16 m.p.g. (same as on petrol); speed, same as on petrol; starting and getting away when warm, very good; starting from cold first thing in the morning, not good, unless doped with petrol. Benzole was 3¾d. cheaper than petrol, taking a quantity in steel casks. Every driver of the firm was told to use benzole, and the principal insisted on having it put in his own car, a 4½ h.p. De Dion.

Encouraged by the tests the Chatterley Coal and Iron Company set about putting the new fuel on the market in Staffordshire and the

33

Thomas Butler, a director of Wm. Butler & Co., bought this 12 h.p. Clement at the Paris Motor Show of 1902. The first car to be registered in Bristol, "AE.1" became well known not only to the public but to the police—a distinction not too desirable in view of the very restricted speed limit. As a benzole distributor, Mr. Butler naturally ran his car exclusively on benzole.

adjoining counties. Meanwhile the Newcastle Benzol Company (Blaydon Benzol) were doing the same thing for the North of England and, with considerable enterprise, actually exporting benzole to France for use in Paris taxicabs. (Presumably it was on benzole that the Parisian taxi established its reputation for homicidal verve.)

In general, however, the individual benzole producer found it hard to compete with the superior distribution of the petrol companies. As the use of neat benzole required an adjustment to the carburettor, the majority of motorists were not prepared to go to this trouble, for they could not always be certain of getting benzole when they wanted it, especially if they travelled outside the distribution area. Needless to say, the petrol companies did not hesitate to make play with this in their propaganda, and the benzole producers found themselves up against a good deal of prejudice.

Despite these difficulties the remarkable properties of the new fuel were gradually becoming more widely known. All those concerned with benzole production were, of course, using it in their own cars and lorries. In 1906 the editor of *The Car* carried out tests on benzole and reported in print that his Daimler "seemed above herself". In the following year its use was officially recommended by the Automobile Association. It was increasingly discussed in the motoring press and amongst discriminating car-owners. Yet so strong was the spirit of commercial individualism in those days that no effort was made by the benzole producers to get together and market this fuel on a national scale, even though it was obvious that none of them on his own could hope to emulate the supply organisation and the nation-wide distribution of the petrol companies.

With the outbreak of war benzole disappeared completely from the motor fuel market. It is a vital ingredient in the manufacture of explosives, and the munitions factories were calling out for every drop of it they could get. And they could not get enough. As the war dragged on many new benzole-producing plants were erected, leading to a vast increase in the country's total benzole production.

Even before the end of the war was in sight some of the benzole producers were beginning to wonder what was to happen to all these expensive new plants when the manufacture of explosives no longer required the vast quantities of benzole they were producing, now far in excess of pre-war demand. The industrial requirements for benzole were a mere prophetic fraction of what they were to become in forty years' time. Unless the surplus could somehow be "unloaded" most of these new plants, equipped at great capital expense, would become idle.

The Five Towns had already played an important part in the benzole story, but now they were to play the leading part in decisions which were to affect the whole future of benzole marketing. Mr Samuel Henshaw, Chairman of the Staffordshire Chemical Company, a benzole producer, saw clearly that the solution to the problem lay in the inevitable post-war demands of the motor fuel market, a market which, though still in its infancy, had already shown every

Mr. Samuel Henshaw, founder of the National Benzole
Company, and its Chairman from 1919 to 1942.

sign of being healthy, vigorous – and extremely thirsty. No concerted
effort had yet been made to sell benzole to that market. The petrol
companies were already well dug in, and ready at the first sign of
danger to close ranks against piratical invaders of what they considered to be their territory. Mr. Henshaw realised that there was
no hope of competing with them unless the benzole producers could

bring themselves to abandon their traditional isolationism, throw their benzole into a common pool and somehow formulate a common marketing policy on a nation-wide scale. He found a firm supporter in Sir David Milne-Watson, and as early as June 1917 a meeting of representatives of the coke oven industry, the tar distillers and some of the gas companies was convened at the Gas, Light and Coke Company headquarters in Westminster.

The petrol companies were, of course, well aware of the problem facing the benzole industry and only too anxious to take over the benzole distribution themselves. The more far-seeing of the producers realised that such an arrangement would in time leave them, individually, at the mercy of the petrol companies, with no price safeguards, and unable to take common action in their own interests. Benzole would become a nonentity. By pooling their production and marketing they would have more control over their produce in the exciting new developments in the fuel market that lay ahead.

At this stage only about 40 per cent. of the producers concerned agreed to come in on the plan to establish a common policy. However, a committee was formed to thrash out details and met at frequent intervals during 1917 and 1918. Sympathetic interest in this plan to market a home-produced fuel was shown by the R.A.C., the A.A. and other motoring organisations, who were often represented at these meetings and indeed actually offered to put up some of the capital (an offer which was gratefully declined).

Four days after the Armistice Mr Henshaw's delicate task of steering so many different manufacturers towards a common end was crowned with success. A resolution was taken to form an association of benzole producers, each participant agreeing not only to pool his benzole production but to refine it to a standard specification. Less than three months later a marketing company was registered, and so, on February 1st 1919, with Mr Henshaw as Chairman, the National Benzole Company was born.

The appearance of "National Benzole" (it was not yet a mixture) thus coincided with the beginning of the great Vintage Era in car design and a great surge forward in the popularisation of the motor car.

CHAPTER 5

The Vintage Era: 1919–1930

(a) *Ordinary Cars*

It might be just as well to get this matter of nomenclature right from the start. *Veteran Cars* include all cars that were built not later than 1904, and it is these which take part in the Veteran Car Run to Brighton (not the "old crocks' race", please: it is not a race, and most of the machines taking part are probably kept in better condition than some contemporary models). *Edwardians* are cars built from 1905 up to the war years. *Vintage Cars* are those which appeared in the decade from the end of the war up to 1930.

This first post-war decade was a vintage period not only for the luxury car and the sports car but for the ordinary car as well. That is not to say that all cars built at this time were perfect: there is many a·disappointing wine in a vintage year that no connoisseur would call a vintage wine. Nevertheless the general standard of design and workmanship during these years was higher than it was to be again for a long time to come (with a few notable exceptions) – until several years after the Second World War, in fact.

The car was still a hand-made, or hand-assembled, job. Designs were based on sound engineering principles, for they were the outcome of something the engineer was trying to make as well as he possibly could, not a compromise attempt to give the salesmen something they imagined the customer wanted. Low top-weight, rigid chassis construction, firm springing, a long wheel base which kept the main weight distribution between the axles, positive steering – all these advantages, compared with the poor design of most of the early mass-production cars of the 1930's, made for better road-holding and safer driving generally, and more than compensated for the trials and discomforts outlined in Chapter 1.

During the war many of the car manufacturers had turned over to making aeroplane engines, and their experience in this field, where lightness of weight and maximum power for the size of the engine were of paramount importance, led to the introduction of light alloys and high-tensile metals in the car engines they began to make when the war was over. The use of aluminium alloy pistons in aeroplane engines enabled piston speeds and power output to be greatly increased. The old slow-turning side-valve engine gave way gradually to the more efficient overhead-valve engine. Aeroplane practice also inspired early post-war experiments with air-cooling for light cars, notably in the Rover "Eight" which appeared in 1919, but the apparently inescapable noisiness of the air-cooled engine was a serious disadvantage, and when light cars began to be manufactured in larger numbers around 1922 they had virtually all returned to the conventional radiator.

The "hand-made" tradition, with its individual approach to engineering problems, was reflected in the quality of material and workmanship that went into every part of the car, even in many of the cheaper range of light cars. When Morris, who had embarked on his fabulous manufacturing career in 1912 with the "Oxford", produced the cheaper "Cowley" version in 1919, there was nothing cheap about the materials or the equipment. For this reason it would put up with any amount of rough treatment or neglect and has survived in considerable numbers to the present day. For a moderately priced light car it had a remarkably quiet engine and smooth gear-change, and these standards were maintained when in the early 'twenties Morris introduced to England the American-type mass-production assembly line and startled the motoring world by reducing the price of all his models by £100 on the eve of the 1921 Motor Show. The "bull-nose" Morris did for England what the Ford Model T did for America and still inspires a similar reminiscent affection. It holds an honourable, though modest, place in the Vintage tradition.

The same high standard of attention to equipment quality and detail was to be found in several other utility cars of the very early 'twenties, notably the Austin 12, the Humber and the Talbot 8/18's, the 11.9 h.p. Lagonda, the Standard Fourteen – though it must be said that the sturdy little Jowett, whose wonderfully reliable twin-cylinder engine was first made in 1910 and continued in production

A mid-'twenties Jowett. These Bradford-manufactured cars were so robustly built that it used to be claimed that every one made since production began in 1919 was still in active use.

basically unchanged until 1952 (an unsurpassed production-run record of 42 years!), did not carry the engine's refinement over into the rest of the car, which was characterised by ugly lines and rough finish.

It was the open touring car, however, with its excellent workmanship, its combination of toughness and elegance, and its generally confident air of "raring to go", which carried forward the pre-war trend of motoring habit and style and might be said to be the most typical car of the early years immediately after the war.

The supreme example was undoubtedly the Sunbeam. Created by a team headed by the brilliant French designer Louis Coatalen, and developed against a background of successful racing experience, the Sunbeam tourers which appeared between 1919 and 1926 reached the summit of Vintage refinement and achievement. Their first post-war models were developments from the pre-war side-valve 3-litre 12/16 which, in a racing version, had swept the board in the 1912 Coupe de l'Auto; the finest of these was the superb 24/60 brought out in 1922. Sunbeams then proceeded to issue a really amazing variety of new models, starting with the "14" and culminating in the 14/40 and the 20/60 of 1925. In 1926, having given birth to the brilliant 3-litre sports car (of which more anon), Coatalen left the firm to return to his native France, and within a few years Sunbeams went into a sad decline which only ended when the company went into liquidation in 1935.

Rolls-Royce, who had since 1906 relied entirely on the already legendary "Silver Ghost", astonished everybody in 1922 by producing the comparatively small "Twenty", which, though a good deal more expensive than the normal tourer, can be considered as belonging

Rolls-Royce's first departure from "The Silver Ghost", the touring "Twenty" first marketed in 1922. This is a 1927 model. Although considerably cheaper than the "Silver Ghost" it was still an exquisitely luxurious car and is naturally one of the most sought-after Vintage tourers.

41

to the touring class of this period. It was, of course, often given dignified saloon coachwork, but it was more attractive in its open version and became one of the most desirable of the Vintage Era tourers for those who wished to travel long distances on continental holidays with a comfortable assurance of utter reliability.

Many motorists of those days will remember the name Crossley with some affection. The $4\frac{1}{2}$-litre of 1908 had done a tremendous job during the war as an ambulance and as a staff car, adding considerable lustre to the Crossley reputation. The 25/30 which came on

Crossleys had a reputation for toughness. These two warriors are seen here with their drivers after a successful Cape-to-Cairo journey in 1925—a gruelling test of a car in those days.

the market in 1919 was virtually the same car, and rivalled the Rolls "Silver Ghost" in longevity by remaining in current production until 1926. Meanwhile in 1920 Crossleys catered for the man of more moderate means by making a capacious 19.6 h.p. tourer, and, in the lighter field, a "Fourteen" which became popular as a modest family touring car. In 1932, at the height of the financial depression, they sadly deserted their Vintage tradition and went in for rather

characterless cars at a much lower price, but after only a few years
of this they lost heart and abandoned the car market for good.

Another car which performed yeoman service during the war was
the D-type Vauxhall, which became a familiar sight as a staff car
on every front from Belgium to the Middle East. It was a Vauxhall
which took King George V to Vimy Ridge in 1917, and it was a
Vauxhall which was the first car to cross the Rhine after the armistice. After the war the firm resumed manufacture with a 25 h.p.
tourer, which is how the D-type had started life in 1912. The
designer, Laurence Pomeroy, was also responsible for the great 30/98
sports car, which went into limited production at about the same
time, and was sometimes to be seen as a "fast tourer" but we shall
hear more about that in a later chapter. In 1922 the D-type tourer
was given overhead valves and other minor modifications and became
the OD-type, or 23/60. This car was a real gentleman; its maximum
speed was only in the region of 65 m.p.h., but it was a delight to

The Vauxhall 23/60 tourer of 1922

handle and remarkably quiet. Like many other manufacturers Vauxhalls soon felt obliged to make a smaller model, and brought out the 14/40 light car which they were to go on producing in fairly large quantities until 1927. In 1925 the concern was acquired by General Motors, who shortly afterwards abandoned production of the 30/98, the 23/60 and the 14/40 in favour of a one-model "family man's car". All that remained of the old Vauxhalls was the name and the fluted bonnet which had been a distinctive feature ever since 1905 and was to continue right up to 1957.

Readers will call to mind many other tourers of the same period. Humber, A.C., Austin, Delage and Bugatti of France, Alfa-Romeo, Lancia and Fiat of Italy – all produced tourers of Vintage quality, and examples of these, along with the Sunbeams and others mentioned above, are now sought after by connoisseurs. Many of them are getting more difficult to find, for the tourer, by its very nature, was a hard-working car which in its advancing years tended to be treated as a maid-of-all-work and kept going until it dropped. The tourer represents what may seem to some a lost golden age, when the weather was apparently kinder and people thought it fun to go off for the day with a car full of family or friends and enjoy the feeling of the sun on the face and the wind in the hair. Nowadays we drive around in our closed saloons, winding up the window lest the breeze should disturb the wife's perm or send a draught down Granny's neck.

The year 1922 must rank as one of the most important in the history of British motoring, for it was in that year that the infant prodigy Austin Seven appeared on the market for the first time.

Herbert Austin began to manufacture cars under his own name in 1905 at Longbridge near Birmingham (one of his first draughtsmen, incidentally, was A. J. Hancock, who left his drawing-board shortly afterwards to become Vauxhall's most successful racing driver). Austin's first car was a fairly large 25–30 h.p. tourer, but during the next few years other models were added to the range. Within five years his payroll had reached 1,000. When car manufacture was resumed after the war he decided to concentrate for the time being on a single model, the Austin "Twenty", a straightforward tourer with no pretensions to beauty but selling at the

44

Lord Brabazon of Tara at the wheel of his 1908 Grand Prix Austin, which is still capable of 85 m.p.h. The occasion was the 21st birthday rally of the Vintage Sports Car Club at Goodwood in 1955.

sensationally low price of £495 compared with £700 for its pre-war counterpart. In normal production trim it had a far from lively performance, but tuned up and stripped down for racing it won quite a reputation at Brooklands in the hands of F. Scriven, once achieving a lap speed of just under 95 m.p.h. Sales of the "Twenty" were good, but the firm was suffering the effects of over-rapid expansion and getting into serious financial difficulty. An official receiver had actually been appointed in 1922 when the new baby car, conceived and designed by Austin himself, ran away to an immediate success against all predictions. The receiver found his services had become redundant, and from that day the company has never looked back.

Someone has described how, when the first "Seven" was ready for its road test, Austin himself "took his place in the driving seat to make the first run. The car started first time, moved briskly out of the shop and snorted happily up the road, the broad shoulders and bowler hat of its creator squarely silhouetted at the helm." He was

One of the great landmarks of British motoring history,
the "Baby" Austin Seven of 1922 which brought mobility to
millions of families.

in fact driving into the dawn of a new era of motoring for everyman
and his family, for though the "Seven" looked rather a frail little
thing it was in fact made of the best materials and very strong. What
is more, though it cost only £225 (and even less as the years went by),
and was less than nine feet long, it was a real car with four seats.
It struck the death-knell of the unlamented cycle-car and made
motoring possible for millions of people who had hitherto never
imagined they would be able to afford it. It had its faults – the
clutch was particularly fierce – but hell! it would tootle along at 45

46

with no trouble at all and even reach 50 if you wanted it to – with a consumption of 45 miles to the gallon. What is more, unlike most of the other cars on the market (Rolls-Royce included), it had four-wheel brakes – quite a thing for 1922.

Few people apart from sports car enthusiasts remember today that the Baby Austin also had a distinguished record on the race track. E. C. Gordon England was quick to appreciate its possibilities, and with numerous subtle modifications to the same basic engine and careful attention to the streamlining of every part of the body, a most

Austin Seven racing cars fighting it out in a 500-mile race at Brooklands. Several supercharged versions of these amazing little cars actually topped the 100 m.p.h. mark.

successful small racing machine was evolved which beat everything in its class with monotonous regularity. What is more, Austin actually listed it and marketed it himself as the "Brooklands" Austin, with a guarantee top speed of over 75 m.p.h. Later he even produced a supercharged "Seven" which developed into, and was catalogued as, the famous "Ulster" Austin, capable of over 80 m.p.h. Amazing what you can do with a baby car when you really try!

Morris Minor open two-seater, selling for well under £200. The Minor formed the basis of the M.G. M-type "Midget".

Austin's success with the "Seven" triggered off a whole spate of cheap light cars, and within a few years you could take your choice of several models selling for under £200 – the best-known of which were the Morris Minor, the Singer Junior, the Triumph Seven, the Standard Nine, the Clyno, the Swift—and of course the Austin Seven, which by 1929 had reduced its price to £125.

A car which was so eccentric that it really formed a category of its own was the Trojan two-stroke light car made by Leyland Motors and popularly known as the "bath on wheels". That is just what it was, for in place of the normal chassis frame it was held together by a large metal box, or steel "punt", in which, sited immediately under the front seats, rested the engine and the gearbox. The back axle was solid, and driven by a long roller chain on the right-hand side of the car. Braking operated on a single drum on the

The Trojan "bath on wheels"

back axle; being the only one this brake-drum had to be pretty powerful, so much so that a too sudden application of the brake pedal was apt to cause the back of the car to part company with the front. Fortunately this operation was rarely necessary, as the car's top speed was 38 m.p.h. Serious production began in 1922, the same year that saw the birth of the Austin Seven. The Trojan was an ingenious attempt to build a really cheap, basic, no-trimmings, foolproof car.

It was alone on the market in having solid tyres, but the customers were so often getting stuck in tramlines that Leylands soon had to change over to the high-pressure pneumatic tyre which was standard on all other cars of the early 'twenties. It was certainly a remarkably trouble-free machine and modest in its fuel consumption, but compared with all its light-car contemporaries it took too long to get anywhere, and in 1929 Leylands stopped making it.

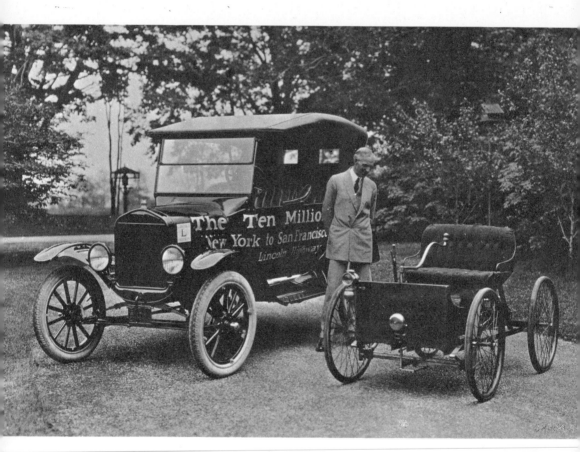

In 1924 the 10,000,000th Model T Ford came off the production line, and here it is alongside the first Ford car ever made, with Henry Ford himself looking modestly on. The first Model T was produced in 1908, and by the time its manufacture ceased in 1927 a total of fifteen million had been sold. It was the first car to be mass-produced in a big way.

W. R. Morris was the first to apply the Ford assembly-line production method to car manufacture in England. As a result he was able to make sensational price reductions for 1922. Here is a 1930 view of part of the Morris works at Cowley, near Oxford.

It is hard for us to realise now that once upon a time there were no such things as halt signs, traffic lights, one-way streets, parking problems – when even Staines bridge had never seen a traffic jam. Nowadays, if we come across a sharp bend or a country cross-road unmarked by a road warning sign, we grumble to our frightened passenger that "they" ought to do something about "that". In the early 'twenties the road was your own, and how you drove on it (providing you did not exceed 20 m.p.h. in the vicinity of a police speed trap) was your own affair; it was up to you to use your own judgment when approaching sharp bends and cross-roads. The modern nightmare of the uninterrupted roar of week-end traffic along the main arteries was still to come. What is more, you could picnic practically anywhere in the country without finding twenty other motorists who had had the same idea: the present conception of the "beauty spot" with its fleet of touring coaches, its ice-cream van, its tea-and-bun stall and its litter basket which no one uses, was a horror undreamt of by those who were sufficiently enterprising to have a car of their own in those days.

Bang in the middle of the road, a Jowett owner enjoys the peaceful seclusion of Box Hill in the late 'twenties.

But every silver lining has its cloud, and we must not forget the thousands of car-less town-dwellers who never had a chance to get away from bricks and mortar and polluted air. It was they who got their opportunity when the Trojan, the Austin Seven and the other cheap light cars came on to the market – and who shall deny any man his right to a place in the sun?

Typical "ordinary" cars of 1925: a 14-h.p. Standard and a 10/23-h.p. Talbot

Cars in the 1926 General Strike. Above, giving lifts to stranded City workers.
Below, Ramsay MacDonald sets off for peace talks at No. 10.

Early filling pumps. Above, a day-and-night filling station of 1921, complete with "floral decoration". Below, filling up from a shilling-in-the-slot pump on the main road beyond Guildford: a useful service for the late-night motorist of the 'twenties.

CHAPTER 6

The Vintage Era (continued)

(b) Luxury Cars

The Rolls-Royce reputation was high enough before 1914, but it emerged from the war enhanced beyond measure. The achievements of the Rolls-Royce staff cars and ambulances on the Western Front, and above all of their armoured cars in the Middle East, have been recounted by Mr Harold Nockolds in his engrossing history of the Rolls-Royce concern, *The Magic of a Name*. These cars often did fantastic mileages of 50,000 or more over appallingly rough country with little or no servicing and were still running as sweetly as ever at the end. At Gallipoli on one occasion two of the armoured cars were reversed – silently, of course – up to the Turkish lines at night, attached by grapnel to the enemy barbed wire and then driven away at top speed, leaving behind them large gaps in the wire through which the infantry were able to attack. Colonel T. E. Lawrence had a fleet of nine Rolls-Royce armoured cars in the later stages of his Arabian campaign and used them to play havoc with the Turkish lines of communication. "Great was Rolls," he wrote in *Seven Pillars of Wisdom*, "and great was Royce! They were worth hundreds of men to us in these deserts."

Before the war, in spite of Charles Rolls's personal enthusiasm for amateur flying (he was killed in a flying accident in 1910), Henry Royce himself had set his face against entering the field of aero-engine manufacture. But the outbreak of hostilities in 1914 changed his mind. Characteristically he buried himself away in a small house at St Margaret's Bay in Kent to concentrate on a new and original

An ironical sidelight on the Russian Revolution. Lenin's personal Rolls-Royce, now a popular exhibit in the Central Lenin Museum in Moscow.

design and six months later the first Rolls-Royce "Eagle" engine was on the test bench. This is not the place to tell the story of what the "Eagle" meant to the R.F.C. pilots of those gruelling days and of the number of their lives saved by its ability to keep their machines flying even when radiator and oil tank had been shot away. Rolls-Royce emerged from the war to find that their quickly established pre-eminence in aero-engine design had served to underline their unchallenged superiority in the motor-engineering world. Fortunately for us all in a later war, Royce now decided he was in the aero-engine business for keeps. It was a pair of Eagles, by the way, which powered the first air crossing of the Atlantic by Alcock and Brown in 1919, using the makers' specified fuel mixture of four-fifths petrol and one-fifth benzole. And it was a Rolls-Royce engine which enabled Britain to win the Schneider Trophy outright in 1931.

The chassis and the car: the legendary 6½-litre six-cylinder overhead-camshaft Hispano-Suiza which startled the motoring world of 1919

Before the war the luxury car was usually chauffeur-driven, and regarded as a vehicle in which dignity, reliability and silence came before speed. The "Silver Ghost's" top speed of 65 m.p.h. was considered fairly dashing. After the war, however, more owners wanted the pleasure of doing their own driving – fewer of them, perhaps, could afford to run a chauffeur – and the result was a growing demand for the elegance to be combined with a more lively performance.

This trend was given an unexpected impetus by a foreign car of original design which was the sensation of the 1919 Motor Show. This was the now famous 6½-litre Hispano-Suiza, of Spanish ancestry but built in France and powered by an engine developed from the wartime aero-engine designed by the Swiss engineer Marc Birkigt. It was so near perfection, so regal in appearance, and so far ahead of its time that for once the Rolls-Royce nose was put out of joint. It had a three-speed gear-box instead of the four-speed box used by nearly every other car of the day; in fact, once the car was moving the driver hardly needed to change gear at all, so flexible and powerful was it in top gear. Yet its maximum speed was somewhere between 75 and 80. It also had four-wheel brakes, operated by a mechanical servo motor driven off the gearbox, a brake-assisting mechanism later adapted by Rolls-Royce and still in use by them today.

The Hispano-Suiza shook the British car manufacturers rigid. Even Rolls-Royce realised that the days of the seemingly eternal "Silver Ghost" were numbered. However, they went on making it for another four years (adding the small "Twenty" in 1922) while Henry Royce closeted himself at his home in West Wittering with his experimental draughtsmen and set to work on the designing of a successor. During 1924 it became known that W. O. Bentley was road-testing the prototype of a new car aimed at the luxury market, and work on the new Rolls-Royce was speeded up accordingly. In 1925 the Phantom was introduced to the public for the first time, and the "Silver Ghost" era had come to an end after a splendid production run of nineteen years. The new Phantom's higher bonnet line gave the car a more powerful appearance than its sedate predecessor, and the new overhead-valve engine provided a maximum speed of

A self-made man who built the aristocrat of motor cars. Sir Henry Royce, born in Lincolnshire in 1863, started work as a newspaper boy for W. H. Smith & Son at Clapham Junction.

Here, at the peak of his success, is Sir Henry at his home at West Wittering, at the wheel of one of the first Phantom I's.

somewhere around the 80 mark while still maintaining the Rolls-Royce tradition of complete silence. For the first time in the company's history four-wheel brakes were fitted as standard, six years after the Hispano-Suiza and three years after the Austin Seven.

Still seeking the greater perfection, Henry Royce designed yet one more car, the Phantom II. Although he was now an invalid and spent his winters in his villa in the South of France, he retained control of the design department at Derby. The Phantom II of 1929, with a top gear performance ranging from dead slow to 85 m.p.h., was the finest car he made, especially in its "Continental" version. In the following year he received a knighthood in recognition of his services to his country during the war and of his great contribution to the reputation of British engineering throughout the world. Sir Frederick Henry Royce, Bt., O.B.E., died in 1933 at the age of seventy. Since that date the initials RR on the radiator badge have been engraved in black instead of red.

Although Bentley aimed his larger cars at the luxury market, and produced his 6½-litre at the Motor Show in the same year as the Phantom I, he never succeeded in establishing a serious rivalry with Rolls-Royce in the purely luxury class. This was due, ironically enough, to the very fame of his successes at Le Mans and elsewhere. For though Bentley rightly maintained that his cars were not racing cars it was their decidedly powerful appearance which tended to confine their appeal to the sporting driver-owner who sought lively performance above all and happened only incidentally to appreciate a high standard of comfort as well. We shall deal in our next chapter more fully with the Bentley as a sports car, but his 1925 6½-litre, the "Speed Six" of 1929 and the 100 m.p.h. 8-litre of 1930 all combined high speed with a remarkable degree of silence and luxurious comfort, and should by rights be accorded a place in the very top rank of luxury cars.

No such sporting "stigma" could be said to have attached itself to the Daimler of this period. It was a rare event to see one without a uniformed chauffeur in the driving seat. The Daimler accent was entirely on dignity, unobtrusiveness and smoothness. It was the perfect car for royal occasions. The Knight double-sleeve-valve

Of these two Daimlers parked together, one is 1911 and the other 1924.
Which is which? Below is a 16-h.p. Daimler of 1925.

engine provided silence but no great power, top gear being designed to give great flexibility rather than high maximum speed. Body design was extremely conservative too, and held fast to the high, upright pre-war styles long after everybody else had brought the roof a good deal nearer the ground. On the other hand the firm was able to offer a surprisingly various range of different models from 12 to 52 h.p.

Dr Lanchester, who, as we saw earlier, built the first British-designed car in 1895, was still going strong (his younger brother, George H. Lanchester, who assisted him in his pioneer work, is still alive today), and the firm continued to produce high-class cars that maintained the Lanchester individualistic tradition of creative engineering. At the Motor Show of 1919 they launched their imposing "Forty", which though overshadowed by the Hispano-Suiza was an advanced car for its time and drove yet another nail

Montagu Napier standing beside his 1919 40/50 luxury tourer

in the ultimate coffin of the Silver Ghost, beating it by 10–15 m.p.h. in top speed and by £50 in price. When Rolls came out with their small "Twenty", Lanchester countered it in the following year with their own "Twenty", again slightly faster and cheaper. Unfortunately the fine 5-litre "Thirty" of 1928 came a little too late, and like many other worthy manufacturers at this time the Lanchester concern foundered in the economic storm of the early 1930's, being absorbed into the B.S.A.–Daimler group. A sad end to a great name in British motoring history.

Two other British cars in the luxury market should be mentioned

Although Napiers ceased to make private cars in 1925, their engines played a prominent part in the record-breaking achievements of the late 'twenties and the 'thirties. Here is a peep under the bonnet of John Cobb's Napier-Railton, in which he was to establish the ultimate Brooklands lap record.

here: the powerful Leyland "Eight" designed by Parry Thomas, whose racing version several times broke the Brooklands lap record, and the 6¼-litre 40/50 which was Napiers' last effort at a private car before they turned over exclusively to making aero-engines. Both these rather heavy cars contained interesting advanced features,

The actual car which won the 1903 Gordon Bennett Trophy took part in a cavalcade of historic cars at Silverstone in 1950.

but somehow they never made much headway and ceased production round about 1925. The withdrawal of Napiers from car manufacture seemed a pity; the sensational day in 1902 when Montagu Napier and S. F. Edge wrested the Gordon Bennett Trophy from the French by their magnificent drive in the marathon race from Paris to Vienna was still remembered, both in England and on the Continent. That Napiers themselves had not forgotten was shown in 1931 when they made a bid to take over Bentley; it is fascinating to speculate on what the outcome of such a partnership might have been if Rolls-Royce had not pipped them on the post.

There will always be room in the luxury market for the unusual car which is different from everybody else's and during the Vintage Era several foreign challengers kept the British manufacturers on their toes, notably Renault, Bugatti, Isotta Fraschini, Duesenberg, Lincoln and Packard. Mercedes produced some expensive cars which made more noise than their performance justified, the noise rising to a piercing scream as the supercharger was brought into play – for not more than 20 seconds at a time, according to the makers' recommendation (and only when using a 50/50 petrol-benzole mixture!).

But by 1930 the heyday of the Vintage luxury car was nearly over. As belts and purse-strings began to be tightened all over the Wall Street dominated world, only the firms with long-established reputations and large capital reserves were able to avoid extinction or absorption.

Ettore Bugatti might be described as the Henry Royce of France. He had a comparable engineering flair and integrity. Unlike Royce, however, he produced a bewildering variety of models and ranged over the whole field of luxury touring, racing and sports cars. Here is the engine of his Type 44 of 1927, which though intended as a tourer was immensely successful in competition and was one of the best cars he ever produced.

CHAPTER 7

The Vintage Era (continued)

(c) Racing and Sports Cars

Something happened in 1911 that was of great significance not only for motor racing but for the development of every type of car. The winner of the French Grand Prix of that year was, as usual, a large car – but second was a "baby" Bugatti, forerunner of the Austin Seven and all the other light cars of the post-war years. The following year in the same race, which was run simultaneously with the Coupe de l'Auto for smaller cars, a sensation was caused when three 3-litre Sunbeams not only finished first, second and third in their own class but were beaten by only two cars in the Grand Prix itself. One of those was a huge 14-litre Fiat, but the winner was a 7½-litre Peugeot, product of the great Swiss designer, Ernest Henry. The Peugeot, with an engine only just over half the size of the Fiat, and the Sunbeams with engines less than a quarter the size, killed once and for all the idea that a car had to be large to be fast.

Henceforward size and brute force were not enough. The future was to be with the designer who by constant improvement of the shape and efficiency of every detail of engine and chassis could extract more power from a given cylinder capacity.

This victory of brain over brawn by Bugatti, Henry and the Sunbeam designer, Louis Coatalen, did it is true foreshadow the end of the awe-inspiring spectacle of thundering contests between the giants. On the other hand it made it more likely that in the future the lessons learnt in racing would be applicable to the design of the ordinary production car. Indeed the Sunbeams were only vamped-up versions of the production side-valve 12/16. It also broke the rich man's monopoly of fast motoring and paved the way for the greater variety and interest of the "Vintage Sports Car".

The "sports car" as such was unknown before 1914, and has in fact never been satisfactorily defined even though we all know one when we see it. The racing car is designed and built specifically for racing; it is not meant to be driven on the road (and is indeed usually impossible to drive in traffic). The sports car, however, is intended to be roadworthy in every respect; it is merely faster, zippier and generally more fun to drive than the normal road car. It developed from the pre-war "fast touring car" which achieved its finest expression in the "Prince Henry" D-type Vauxhall, the car that was used as a staff car during the war and in 1919 developed into the superlative 30/98 "Velox" (not to be confused with recent models of the same name) which set the tone for the "sports car" of the Vintage Era. The 30/98 did not, for various reasons, play a great part in competitive events —it was intended as a "sporting car" rather than as a "sports car"— but in its overhead-valve version it was guaranteed by the makers to lap Brooklands at 100 m.p.h., and the story goes that customers would sometimes take delivery at the track after proof of guarantee. The Vauxhall 30/98, designed by Laurence Pomeroy, was one of the great cars of all time – its supremacy in the sporting-touring field during the Vintage years being threatened only by a man who produced his first car in that same year of 1919.

W. O. Bentley's single-minded determination to make fast cars of superb quality succeeded in putting Britain's name on the highest level of international sports-car racing. After twelve years of precarious existence on insufficient capital, his company ran full tilt into the 1931 slump and was forced into liquidation. But during those years he produced a series of powerful sports cars which, in the hands of Henry Birkin, Woolf Barnato, Glen Kidston, and the rest of the "Bentley Boys", won remarkable victories on the race track and took the chequered flag at Le Mans no fewer than five times. The Bentley car became a kind of symbol of the Vintage Era.

Before the war "W.O." had acquired the British concession for a little-known French car, the D.F.P. Even in those days he showed his faith in racing as the best form of publicity, for with a tuned-up

The pinnacle of Vintage Sports Car design, the Vauxhall OE 30/98. Strangely enough this immortal car might never have come about if it had not been for an amateur sporting motorist called J. Higginson, who in 1913 asked Vauxhalls to build for him, at rather short notice, a special car suitable for hill-climbs. The result, designed by Laurence Pomeroy and based on the Vauxhall D-type tourer, was exactly what Higginson asked for and was virtually the prototype of the 30/98 which Vauxhalls put into production in 1919–20. In 1922 the side-valve engine was given push-rod overhead valves and became the OE type pictured here.

engine he entered for a large number of competitive events, starting with the Aston hill-climb, which he won, beating several class lap records at Brooklands and making an honourable showing in the 1914 Isle of Man International T.T. The secret of his success lay in the increase of piston speed afforded by aluminium alloy pistons. When the war came Bentley tried to convince the Service engineers of their value, and after some initial scepticism aluminium pistons were adopted for the new aero-engines being made by Rolls-Royce, Sunbeam and others. Working in co-operation with Humbers Bentley also designed and developed the successful Bentley Rotary aircraft engine.

The war over, "W.O." set about building a car to his own design, and despite the inevitable post-war material shortages he had the first engine ready on the test bench by October 1919. It is amusing, in the context of this book, to learn that the engine failed to start first time on ordinary petrol. "I won't linger," Bentley wrote in his autobiography, "over the awful anxiety while Clarke tested the valve timing and fiddled with the carburettor. Benzole did the trick—and at once the three-inch exhaust was bellowing and the straight-tooth gears screaming with enough noise to awaken the dead." So far so good, but he still had to build a chassis to put the engine into, and the Motor Show was only a month away. Nevertheless a mock-up 3-litre Bentley made its bow at Olympia on time, caused considerable interest and brought orders. The difficulty then was to get the car into production, and as the infant company was working on little more than a shoestring and the smell of many oil rags it was not until September 1921 that the first production car was delivered to a customer.

Deriving its inspiration partly from the Mercedes which had swept the board in the 1914 Grand Prix, and partly from a Peugeot racing 3-litre, the Bentley was the first road car to incorporate the main features of pre-war racing practice. With its overhead valves (four to each cylinder) rocker-operated by a central bevel-driven camshaft, the four-cylinder engine was capable of pushing the car along at a maximum speed of 75 m.p.h. or more and had no trouble at all in cruising at 65 for hours on end. It could go for long periods without servicing, and at 30 m.p.h. it would do 30 miles to the gallon. Needless to say, it had aluminium pistons.

The first experimental 3-litre Bentley of 1919

An early Bentley success at Brooklands. W. G. Barlow after winning the 90-m.p.h. Short Handicap in 1922.

The R.A.C. restarted the Isle of Man Tourist Trophy in 1922 and Bentley entered a team of three cars, one of which he drove himself. They caused something of a stir by gaining second, fourth and fifth places. Two years later a privately entered 3-litre Bentley, driven by Duff and Clement, came in first at Le Mans in the twenty-four hour endurance race for sports cars in standard road trim which had been inaugurated the previous year.

Meanwhile Bentley was working on the design of a new car, the experimental prototype being built as a $4\frac{1}{4}$-litre. The reason for its ultimate enlargement into a $6\frac{1}{2}$-litre was an extraordinary coincidence which occurred while the heavily disguised prototype was returning from its extended road-testing on the long straight roads of France. The incident has been beautifully described by Bentley himself in his autobiography, *W.O.*:

We caught sight of another car, as unusual as ours, converging on our Route Nationale and trailing a cloud of dust. It was going very fast and which of us was going to get to the Y junction ahead first appeared questionable. The arrival was in fact simultaneous, with neither of us giving way to the other.

The car I now recognised as a Rolls-Royce, but like no Rolls I had seen before – until I remembered that the company had produced their prototype Phantom I o.h.v. car at almost the same time as we completed the experimental six-cylinder. By an extraordinary coincidence we had crossed one another's tracks on our proving trials at the same moment in the centre of the vast land-mass of France; and in spite of our camouflage we had been identified after a quick suspicious glance by their crew as readily as we had recognised them.

This was not a chance to be missed. I put my foot flat on the floor, and the speedometer needle of the $4\frac{1}{4}$, which had been showing a cruising speed of around 65 m.p.h., leapt up towards the eighties. The Rolls driver took similar measures – and along we went, continuing side by side between the poplars on the deserted road, for mile after mile, neither car giving an inch to the other, up the hills and down the other side.

There was not a half-mile an hour between us, and I suppose we should have continued like this all the way to the Channel coast if the cap of one of the Rolls' crew hadn't blown off and gone spinning away into the dust cloud in our wake, obliging them to pull up after a dozen or so miles. . . .

The result of this unforeseen trial of strength was a decision to step up the power of the engine and when the new $6\frac{1}{2}$-litre appeared it was

The famous incident of the multiple crash at "White House" turn in the early stages of the 1927 Le Mans 24-hour race. F. Gordon Crosby's painting shows the scene of wreckage lit up in the headlights of No. 3 Bentley as it came round the bend too fast to avoid its own collision — the overturned French car on its side across the road, No. 2 Bentley reared up with its one remaining headlamp pointing skywards like a searchlight, and another Bentley impaled in the roadside fence. It looked like disaster for the Bentley team until No. 3 managed to extricate itself and continue the race.

in fact faster than the Rolls-Royce. It was, however, intended as a fast luxury car and, for the time being at any rate, took no part in the Bentley racing programme.

Encouraged by the Duff and Clement win at Le Mans in 1924, Bentley entered a works team in the following year. Bad luck, with every car retiring for trivial defects, dogged the team that year, in which Sunbeams made their first and only appearance at Le Mans and gained second place with one of their new 3-litre sports cars, the only British car to finish. Bentleys were out of luck again in 1926. But next year they figured in one of the most extraordinary races in the whole history of "Les Vingt-Quatre Heures du Mans".

The team this time consisted of two 3-litres and one of the first models of a new 4½-litre. Soon after dusk on the first day a French Schneider came to grief at "White House" turn and lay slewed across the narrow road. The 4½ Bentley, following it round the fast bend, was unable to avoid running into the damaged car. Before anybody could warn them, the two Bentley 3-litres also crashed into the wreckage. No one was hurt, but it was a monumental pile-up and looked like the end of the Bentley challenge so far as this race was concerned. But one of the 3-litres, No. 3 (still known as "Old Number Seven" from its previous year's number), was somehow dragged clear and, though badly damaged, driven slowly on to the

"Old Number Seven" at the pits after the White House crash, with Bentley himself (immediately over the bent wing) ruefully surveying the damage.

Bentley pit where it was patched up and continued the race. The drivers (S. C. H. Davis and Dr Benjafield) settled down in the darkness to face the seemingly impossible task of keeping the car going for the remaining 18½ hours of the race with one headlight smashed, a bent front axle and other damage to the chassis. Miraculously the battered machine kept plugging steadily along, catching up on one car after another until with three hours to go only Chassagne's Aries remained in front. Soon afterwards the Aries came to a standstill with camshaft trouble, and "Old Number Seven" hobbled past it (at 60 m.p.h.) to gain a dramatic victory.

The 1928 win, this time by the 4½-litre which had been the first of the Bentleys to crash at White House the year before, was scarcely

A great moment for Britain. A line-up of the Bentleys which took first, second, third and fourth places in the 1929 Le Mans. The facing page shows the winning car in the course of the race.

less dramatic, with "Babe" Barnato driving the last three laps with a cracked frame and no water, almost neck and neck with the American Stutz with a stripped gear.

The Bentley entry for 1929 included three 4¼-litres and the new "Speed Six", a development from the 1925 6½-litre luxury car. The race was something of a walk-over for the Bentley team, the "Speed Six" driven by Barnato and Birkin heading a leisurely procession over the finishing line for a 1–2–3–4 win. It was the most overwhelming British victory in motor racing to date, and raised the prestige of British cars abroad to a height it had never reached before and was not to approach again for a quarter of a century.

In the following year, 1930, he clinched that great win with yet another Le Mans victory, his fourth in succession. The race was memorable for a great duel between Barnato in a "Speed Six" and the great German driver Caracciola in a 7½-litre supercharged

Mercedes-Benz, the cars passing and repassing each other in truly
thrilling fashion. The duel was part of the Bentley strategy of over-
pressing the Mercedes in the early stages of the race. Eventually the
Mercedes was forced to withdraw with electrical troubles, and two
Bentley "Speed Sixes" went on to take first and second places in a
fairly leisurely manner.

Le Mans 1930. Bentleys take first and second places in their last appearance
in this event. On the right is Woolf Barnato with the winning "Speed Six".
In the following year Bentley sold out to Rolls-Royce, but his Le Mans
successes are still remembered in France.

That was Bentley's last appearance at Le Mans. He produced one more brilliant car, the 8-litre, but it came too late to prevent the firm's imminent demise. Under Rolls-Royce control the Bentley became respectable and took no further part in the racing scene.

The other great British name in racing during the first half of the Vintage decade was undoubtedly that of Sunbeam, though the designer responsible for its policy was a Frenchman, the brilliant Louis Coatalen who had joined the firm in 1909 and within five years made it famous throughout the racing world.

During the war the factory turned over to making very fine aero-engines. In 1919, while Rolls-Royce (as we have seen) had the honour of providing the engine for the Alcock and Brown transatlantic flight, it was Sunbeams who manufactured the engines (and even the pro-pellers) of the British airship R.34 which made a double crossing of

Henry Segrave in a 1921 1½-litre Talbot-Darracq after winning the 200-mile race at Brooklands.

the Atlantic in the same year. A few months later they took the ill-fated step, as it turned out, of amalgamating with the French Talbot-Darracq combine, the new company bearing the uninspiring title of S.T.D. Motors Ltd. The three partners continued to race and sell their cars under their original names. For the next ten years Sun-beams virtually carried the relatively unsuccessful Talbot-Darracq end of the business on their shoulders. After Coatalen's retirement

77

through ill-health in 1926, Sunbeams ceased to build for the future and rested more and more on their past laurels. With that and the economic depression they went into a decline which ended in 1935 with the break-up of S.T.D., and the Sunbeams' and Talbots' absorption into the Rootes organisation.

Throughout the early part of the Vintage Era, however, the Sunbeam reputation shone high in the motor-racing firmament. Like Bentley, Coatalen was a great believer in the advertising value of racing. But whereas Bentley would build a car and then try to sell it by showing what it could do on the track in carefully selected production car events, Coatalen's policy was to build cars especially for racing and to put the experience gained under the gruelling test of competition into the production cars of the future.

Which policy was right is arguable. Coatalen's famous 3-litre of 1925, the first production car ever offered with a twin-overhead-camshaft engine, was a considerable advance on the Bentley 3-litre; but by that time the Bentley was so well established that the Sunbeam salesmen found difficulty in competing with it. The

The engine of "HW 7813", one of the 3-litre Sunbeams shown on the opposite page, recently overhauled by its owner.

Bentley had already proved its paces, but the Sunbeam 3-litre only had a win in the 1927 Essex Six Hours Race at Brooklands (incidentally beating the Bentley team), a second place at Le Mans and one or two minor events at Southport and Blackpool to its credit. And by that time Bentley had already put *his* racing experience into the design of his next car.

But the list of successes gained by the various Sunbeam racing models during the years of Coatalen's reign (and by the same cars for some years afterwards) in continental Grand Prix and in innumerable races, hill-climbs, handicaps and reliability trials at Brooklands and elsewhere, is positively staggering. They regularly swept the board in most of the events they were entered for. In 1923 a Sunbeam 2-litre 6-cylinder, driven by the up-and-coming Henry Segrave, was the first British car ever to win the French Grand Prix – or indeed any Grand Prix – and Sunbeams also took second and fourth places. Sunbeams were all set for a walk-over win in the same race in the following year; unfortunately they were persuaded to fit new but (as it transpired later) defective Bosch magnetos, on the very eve of

A pride of racing Sunbeams:

Left: Sir Algernon Guinness at the wheel of a 1922 T.T. Sunbeam.

On facing page:
1. A 6-cylinder Sunbeam at the start of a 1922 Brooklands 100-m.p.h. Long Handicap.

2. A 4-cylinder 2-litre Sunbeam, with Segrave and his mechanic Moriceau, at Strasbourg in 1922.

3. The 2-litre 1924 supercharged Grand Prix Sunbeam known as "The Cub", seen at a Jubilee Meeting at Brooklands in 1957.

1

3

2

81

The 6-cylinder 3-litre Sunbeam driven by J. Chassagne and S. C. H. Davis which finished second at Le Mans in 1925. It was the only British car to finish.

the race, with the result that despite making the fastest lap the cars suffered from perpetual misfiring and gradually dropped behind. We have already noted their one and only attempt at Le Mans in 1925 when they gained second place. But perhaps they made their greatest impression on the non-technical general public by the part they played in raising the world land-speed record to a height which in 1919 would have been regarded as being beyond the bounds of credibility.

In 1919, astonishingly enough, the record still stood at the 127.66 m.p.h. established by the Stanley steam car in 1906 — in one direction only: by 1919 an average of two runs in opposite directions was required. It was not until May 1922 that K. Lee Guiness took a Sunbeam, fitted with a 350 h.p. 12-cylinder aero-engine, to Brooklands and achieved a new world record of 133.75 m.p.h. (only six miles an hour faster than the steam car sixteen years earlier!). This was the first time the record had been held by Great Britain, and since then only once has a driver of any other country succeeded in wresting it from us.

In 1924 E.A.D.Eldridge, driving a Fiat fitted with a $21\frac{1}{2}$-litre aeroplane engine, put the record up to 146 m.p.h. on a French road. This was the last time the record was set up on a road, and thereafter record-breaking attempts were to be made on salt beds or flat stretches of hard sand. Those who have driven at even 100 m.p.h. on, say, the Hog's Back in the early hours of the morning will appreciate what an alarming experience Eldridge's road speed of half as much again must have been—even on a straight, wide, poplar-lined French road.

In 1923 Malcolm Campbell had acquired from Sunbeams the same 350 h.p. 12-cylinder which Lee Guiness had used for his record-breaking in the previous year. On Saltburn Sands in Yorkshire, and again at Fanoe Island in Denmark, Campbell actually improved on Guiness's record, but the international body responsible for regulating these things refused to recognise his speeds as official because they had not approved the timing apparatus used. He was also having a good deal of trouble with tyres flying off at these high speeds, but eventually Dunlop evolved a special set of wheels and tyres using the "well base" principle on which all car wheels and tyres are made today – yet another instance of the ordinary car benefiting from the experience gained in racing and record-breaking. Racing, as the saying goes, improves the breed – and is still doing so today.

In 1925 Campbell took his Sunbeam to Pendine Sands in South Wales and just managed to top the 150 mark with a mean speed of 150.87 over the two runs. This time there was no mistake over the timing apparatus, and the record qualified for official recognition. But it was not to stand for long.

Coatalen had just completed a new 4-litre 12-cylinder supercharged Sunbeam, and Segrave decided to have a go at Campbell's record on the seven-mile stretch of sand on Southport beach. Things did not go at all smoothly in the practice runs. First the supercharger would not stand the strain, and then Segrave had an alarming experience which required every ounce of coolness he could muster. At the end of the measured mile the throttle jammed in the full open position. Simple enough, you would think, to switch off the ignition. But

Henry Segrave and the 4-litre 12-cylinder Sunbeam in
which he recorded 152.31 m.p.h.

the mechanics had moved the switch since the previous run, and the
dashboard was out of sight behind the streamlining leather cockpit
cover. He was two miles further on and travelling rather fast when
he managed to find the switch and pull up just in time to avoid running out of beach. On the day of the actual attempt the supercharger
gave up the ghost shortly before the end of the second run, robbing
Segrave of the mile record, but he had completed the kilometre and
achieved a new record speed of 152.31 m.p.h.

Another well-known driver now decided to join in the game of
leapfrog. Parry Thomas, with his huge Leyland Eight (a racing version of the luxury car he had designed for Leylands) and his extremely
low "flat-iron" Thomas Specials, was a familiar and popular figure

84

at Brooklands, where in 1925 he established a lap record of 129.36 m.p.h. In 1926 he acquired from Count Zborowski his "Higham Special", a 27-litre aero-engined monster which, though the largest car ever seen at Brooklands, was always at a disadvantage on its constricted layout for that reason. Thomas carried out considerable modifications on this car, christened it "Babs" and in April 1926 took it to Pendine Sands to attack Segrave's record. At one stroke he pushed the record up by nearly twenty miles an hour, achieving a mean average of 171 m.p.h.

Later that year Malcolm Campbell, not in his Sunbeam this time

Parry Thomas at the wheel of his record-breaking "Babs". Note the chain-drive, the cause of his death on his final attempt.

Parry Thomas in "Babs", practising at Brooklands for his first
attempt on the world record at Pendine Sands, April 1926.

but in a new car powered by a Napier aero engine, raised that figure
by a narrow margin. Thomas determined to have another go. In
the middle of his run one of the driving chains snapped and flew up,
killing him instantaneously, and so died one of the great figures of
motor-racing.

Meanwhile Coatalen and Segrave had been hatching a conspiracy
to have done with this nibbling at the record and to go flat out for the
200. It was thought that it would be comparatively inexpensive to
link two existing Sunbeam "Matabele" aero-engines, totalling 1,000
h.p., at opposite ends of a huge chassis frame. If successful it would
gain immense world-wide publicity for the Sunbeam name at a small

fraction of the cost of a season's racing. Perhaps conspiracy is the wrong word, for even when the design was still on the drawing board Coatalen was bold enough to announce publicly that he expected the car to achieve 200 m.p.h.

Neither Pendine nor Southport had a long enough runway for such a speed, nor was there a suitable beach anywhere else in the British Isles or indeed in Europe. So the great machine, with its streamlined shell of advanced design, was taken over to Florida, where at a place called Daytona there was a perfect stretch of over twenty miles of straight flat sand. Running on a set of tyres especially constructed for the operation by Dunlop, who guaranteed they would last for $3\frac{1}{2}$ minutes at 200 m.p.h., Segrave did two runs in opposite directions before a crowd of 15,000, many of whom had camped out

Henry Segrave at the wheel of the 1,000-h.p. aero-engined Sunbeam

on the spot all night, and clocked up an average of 203.79 m.p.h. at his first attempt. The date was March 29th 1927. The magic figure had been reached, and most people thought the ultimate in land speed had now been achieved. Twenty years later the figure was almost doubled.

87

Meanwhile in the following year several challengers came to Daytona to attack Segrave's record. First Campbell nudged it up to 206.96. Then the American designer Frank Lockhart tried in his Stutz, but ploughed into the sea when he was travelling at about 200 m.p.h., fortunately without serious damage to car or driver. Next another American, Ray Keech, drove a vast 4-ton car called the White-Triplex, powered by three aero-engines, at a new record speed of 207.55 m.p.h. Lockhart, having recovered from his earlier mishap, tried again, but this time he was killed when the Stutz burst a tyre and somersaulted several times along the beach.

Once again Segrave showed his dislike of half measures. He came back to Daytona in 1929 in a new Napier-engined car, which he called the Golden Arrow, and hi-jacked the record up to 231.44 m.p.h. He was knighted when he got back to England. In the same year he was killed in the very act of recapturing the world water speed record for Britain.

The lure of speed was beginning to claim its victims. At Daytona the monster White-Triplex, driven this time not by Ray Keech, who had decided the car was too dangerous and sensibly refused to have any more to do with it, but by another American driver, Lee Bible, overturned when it was doing about 200 m.p.h., killing Bible and smashing itself to pieces.

So in 1930, at the end of the Vintage Era, the world land speed record stood at what seemed the fantastic figure of 231.44 m.p.h. set up by Segrave. Malcolm Campbell, however, was convinced that a speed of 300 m.p.h. was attainable and, as we shall see, soon set about trying to prove it.

The pursuit of the world speed record had been followed with enthusiasm by everybody who could read a newspaper, but it had apparently moved far beyond the powers of the ordinary racing car or sports car. So although it is true up to a point that designers had discovered that a car did not have to be large to be fast, it all depends on what you mean by "fast". The last time the record had fallen to a "normal" car was Segrave's 152.33 m.p.h. in 1926. It is interesting to speculate on what might have happened if Lockhart had not been killed when he was attempting the record in his Stutz, for on his first run he had exceeded 200 m.p.h.—and his engine was a mere 3-litre! Had he lived this great American designer might have proved that much greater speeds were possible with an engine of comparatively modest capacity. Meanwhile designers watched the record attempts with interest but abandoned the field to the specialized monsters with their aircraft engines, and confined their attention to improving the sports car and the racing car.

In this chapter we have concentrated on the Sunbeams, the Bentleys and the Vauxhall 30/98 because they were the outstanding cars of the Vintage Era in their particular spheres. In a book of this scope it is not possible to deal in such detail with the many competition

Not in the top class, but great fun for the amateur enthusiast. The "Le Mans" start of a Junior Car Club high-speed reliability test at Brooklands in the 'twenties. The ladies seem to be suffering from an unfair sartorial handicap.

Above: Another view of a Brooklands high-speed reliability trial, with a Frazer Nash leading the competitors down the test hill.

Facing: Exterior view of the Bugatti Type 44 whose engine is shown on page 66. This 3-litre could be had in saloon, coupé, or touring versions and was remarkably quiet even at its maximum speed of 80 m.p.h.

cars that were made during these years, but the period was rich in interesting and excellent examples. Amongst purely racing cars only Sunbeams could put up any kind of a show against the continental Ballots, Bugattis, Delages, Alfa-Romeos and Fiats (the Mercedes domination was still to come), but in the sports car field Britain could boast in addition to Bentley a remarkable variety of celebrated names – Alvis, Riley, Talbot (the Roesch variety), Aston Martin, Invicta, Frazer Nash, M.G., Lagonda . . . Foreign competitors included the Bugattis and the Lancias, but the Continent could offer nothing like the profusion of types of sports car that was to be found in England during the heyday of the Vintage Era.

A pipe of tobacco, a glass of beer in the sun, and a Vintage car—what more
could a man want? On the left is an early M.G., with its parent's bull-nose,
and on the right a rare H.E.

On facing page: A pair of 1923 Aston Martins. *Above:* The side-valve "Green
Pea", well known to Brooklands enthusiasts. *Below:* The famous "Razor
Blade", one of the narrowest racing cars ever built.

A 1930 "Interceptor" Frazer Nash cornering in the best "Nash" manner
at a recent Vintage Sports Car Club event at Prescott.

CHAPTER 8

The Pirates of Horseferry Road

Such, then, was the motoring scene in 1919 and the exciting decade that followed. The Motor Car had arrived, it was becoming a part of everyday life, and its progress along the roads of England was no longer accompanied by ribaldry or sceptical curiosity. More people were beginning to own a car, and with the general introduction of cheap light models around 1922 motoring for the million had become a realisable possibility. And all these thousands of new cars were needing fuel. There could hardly have been a more propitious year than 1919 for the introduction of a new motor spirit.

So, though the sea was rough, seething with turbulent cross-currents and full of uncharted shoals, at the least the wind was fair when, on February 1st 1919, the good ship National Benzole was launched, its skull-and-crossbones flag flying defiantly at the masthead. The petrol companies were well established in the motor spirit market, with distributing organizations covering the whole of the British Isles. This serious attempt to put benzole on the map was rightly recognised as a formidable threat, and the National Benzole pioneers were under no illusions about the uphill struggle ahead of them. But it was a time when piracy was in the air. There were pirate buses plying for custom in the London streets. A man could still make a million with a good idea, hard work and a little bit of luck. You could have an enormous amount of fun being an outsider and trying to punch your way in.

It was this piratical spirit that inspired the handful of staff as they settled down to their difficult task in those early months and helped them to endure the discomforts and minor irritations that are inevitable under "shoestring" conditions. Though the Company started with a capital of half a million, Mr Henshaw, as chairman, realised that the only hope of competing with the oil companies was to keep distribution costs as low as possible, and determined to hold overheads down to the minimum until the firm was more established.

The first office was a room ten foot square in the headquarters of the Gas, Light & Coke Company in Horseferry Road, Westminster. It contained four small tables, a few chairs and a telephone. It was very dark, and artificial light had to be on all the time. The view from the small window was depressing in the extreme: a dismal yard in the foreground, gas-holders towering beyond. All day they had to endure incessant clanging, hissing and hammering from the adjoining boilerhouse, and the constant procession of horse-drawn, iron-tyred vehicles passing immediately outside the window filled the room with maddening surges of clatter and rattle. The atmosphere was permeated by gas. In high summer the heat made the stifling conditions in this crowded little room almost unbearable, and at least one member of the staff remembers taking his desk outside when things got too impossible and sitting in his shirt-sleeves in the welcome shade of the gas-holders.

In these unsalubrious surroundings they began the enormous task of building up the nucleus of a distributing organisation. Not one of them had ever had any experience of this sort of thing before. Henshaw had sworn he would never have an "oil man" in the place. They had to find out as they went along, and improvisation was the order of the day.

At first, until storage depots were set up in various parts of the country, orders were simply passed on to the nearest benzole producer with available supplies, though on occasion this might mean that a customer in Penzance would have his order delivered from somewhere as far away as Durham. One of the great difficulties in those days of post-war shortage was to get enough containers to put the benzole in, nor were National Benzole Company alone in finding themselves up against this problem. One of the big benzole producers in the North, not yet a member of the new association, wrote a letter in the motoring press in June 1919 on the subject: "At the moment we have orders on our books about two months old. Although most of

Mr. Albert Hittinger, who joined the National Benzole Company as Accountant in 1919 and became successively Secretary, General Manager, Managing Director, Deputy Chairman and finally, in 1948, Chairman, a post he held until his retirement in 1955.

these could be executed quickly from benzole in stock, we are prevented from doing so by delays on the part of customers and railway companies in returning the empty packages. . . . Motor traders as a whole are anxious to avoid the benzole getting into the hands of the petrol people. The negligence in attending to the prompt return of empties is forcing benzole makers to put some of their benzole into the hands of the petrol people, who are able to remove it from the works in tank wagons."

Fortunately for the National Benzole Company, a lucky purchase of a large government war-disposal stock of 50-gallon drums and 2-gallon and 4-gallon cans solved their problem for the time being. Then, having got the drums and cans, how to get them to the retailers? There were no great road tankers such as we know today. There was in fact no way of delivering motor spirit in bulk and, even if there had been, the garages had no means of accepting bulk delivery, for there were no storage tanks or roadside pumps. It had to be transported in the drums and cans – by lorry, van or horse and cart. And in 1919 every form of transport was in short supply. Here again the War Disposals Board came to the rescue with a number of lorries which had, from the look of them, seen a good deal of war service.

So indeed had some of the drivers who were taken on by the company – which was just as well, perhaps, since it would come as no surprise to them that these early lorries had open cabs, with no windscreens or side curtains, and provided no protection for the driver beyond a somewhat ineffective apron that was supposed to fit under his chin like a baby's bib. One of the area transport managers was horrified when, as the first winter approached, the drivers asked for windscreens to be fitted in view of the long journeys they often had to undertake. He was "an army man himself", and if the army could do without them so could his drivers. Needless to say, this spartan state of affairs did not last long.

Among the first vehicles owned by the firm was a Model T Ford, which appears to have etched itself in the memory of one of the early members of the staff on account of the day when the bottom of the car fell out and deposited on the road a noisy trail of empty spirit cans, spanners, jacks and other miscellaneous tools. The company also had a horse and cart. Unfortunately the horse chose to go lame on an occasion when one of the order clerks, observed to be idle for once, had been told to "go out and sell some benzole" and returned to everybody's surprise with an order for 1,000 gallons provided it was delivered that afternoon. For want of a horse the order was lost; and it seems that National Benzole lost, not only the order but an obviously potential salesman, for the embittered clerk vowed never to leave his desk again.

In fact they had virtually no salesmen in the first early months. The lorry-drivers did most of the selling – and the account-collecting too. The drill was to load up with as many cans as the lorry would hold, and then to drive off, in a different direction each day, calling on known or potential customers until the whole load was sold and collecting the cash for previous deliveries at the same time. It was nothing unusual for drivers to have a working day of twelve hours or more – one of them remembers frequently setting off at seven in

One of the early National Benzole lorries, *after* windscreens had been fitted. Note the tyres.

the morning and not returning until eleven at night. It must not be forgotten that these lorries rode on solid tyres and had to contend with the rough highway surfaces of those days, quite apart from floods, snowdrifts, landslides and other natural hazards, which caused far more dislocation than they do today. Moreover the lorries were always breaking down, and it was a common occurrence to receive a phone call from one of the drivers to say "the —— piece of string had gone and bust", leaving him stranded in some outlandish spot or other.

99

By the spring of 1920 things were looking up. The head office had found more congenial premises at No. 30 Grosvenor Gardens near Victoria Station. Divisional offices had been set up in Darlington, Manchester, Sheffield, Birmingham and other important towns. More up-to-date lorries were being added to the transport fleet, which now numbered about fifty vehicles. The lorry drivers' work had been lightened by the engagement of proper sales representatives who drove around in Morris Cowleys painted the conspicuous chrome yellow which National Benzole had adopted as their distinguishing colour; this certainly gave the cars considerable advertising value, but proved a slight handicap in collecting overdue accounts, for the customer could see them coming a mile off and arrange to be conveniently "out" by the time they arrived.

Supply depots had been established in a number of key centres. These depots consisted of several hundreds of drums of various shapes and sizes and were often situated in odd corners made available by the benzole producers at their works. The clerical work sometimes had to be done in conditions which made the original head office in Horseferry Road seem like a palace. With a tarpaulin for a roof, rain seeping in to saturate the papers and form pools on the floor, no electric light, no heating in winter – depot life in that first year was no picnic. At one depot the only approach road was across a field and then down a steep incline, the ascent of which in winter with a full load was enough to make even a lorry driver swear. In another depot the drums were stored in vaults below a quayside road, with no windows and no lighting, so that you had to take a miner's safety lamp with you to avoid the pot-holes full of stagnant water. Yet another had its offices on top of a benzole storage tank, with a vent pipe sticking up through the floor.

Due partly to the endeavours of all these heroes, partly to the railway strike of 1919 which had induced motorists to take their cars into the cities and towns in unprecedented numbers, and partly to the increasing number of cars coming on the market, sales of National Benzole were going very well. The pirate motor spirit was certainly making headway, despite the efforts of the petrol companies to throw them off balance by making overnight price reductions and spreading stories that benzole caused cylinder corrosion and other ghastly troubles. Motorists were finding out for themselves that the claims made in the National Benzole advertising were fully justified: "Greater power – increased mileage – sweeter running – absence of knocking in the engine – fewer gear changes."

The new spirit was given a great boost by the result of an official A.A. reliability trial carried out in October 1919. A Sunbeam running on National Benzole was driven ten thousand miles with the specific object of testing the suitability of benzole as a motor fuel. An account of the trial is on record: .

Under close official observation the car left the Sunbeam works at Wolverhampton on August 28th 1919 and proceeded to London. The next day it went north to Inverness, and then south to the Midlands and Eastern Counties. It then proceeded west to Land's End, which it reached on September 19th. Finally it arrived at Maidenhead, from which centre various journeys were made to complete the mileage.

During this historic trial the great railway strike of 1919 occurred. This rendered the task of the drivers more difficult and arduous, by reason of the cutting up of the road surfaces. The heavy burden of the additional transport which the roads had to carry as the result of the strike cut them up into a mass of potholes and ruts. These conditions, needless to say, imposed an additional strain on the car which had not been anticipated.

The run was, however, successfully concluded. It proved for all time the claims made for National Benzole as a motor fuel, and the story was published in the motor papers with sensational effect.

In the following year the company decided to enter for the Dewar Trophy, awarded each year by the R.A.C. for "the most meritorious performance made under the regulations for R.A.C. certified trials." They succeeded in winning the award with a 10,000-mile reliability trial in a 1915 Rolls-Royce 40/50 h.p. open tourer running entirely on National Benzole. It was a great feather in their cap, for since its inception in 1906 the Trophy had never before been awarded to a motor spirit company. The achievement caused a considerable stir in the motoring world.

The railway strike of 1919 had, as we have seen, stimulated the public's use of motor fuel, and benzole had its full share of this increase in demand. Unfortunately the coal strike which began in September of 1920, and lasted through the winter and spring until June of the following year, had a serious effect on benzole production. Only a trickle of coal was reaching the coke ovens at steel and gas works. Although more benzole producers had been coming in (over half the producers in the country were now members of the association), the stocks of benzole began to run down at an alarming rate.

This was a desperate situation for the new firm, a bolt from the blue when all had seemed set fair. They were running into the same difficulty that had dogged the sporadic benzole marketing before the war. The demand for National Benzole was snowballing steadily, and even when the coal strike was settled and the coke ovens returned to their normal output of their benzole by-product it was still not enough. Motorists were complaining loudly about the inadequacy of supplies, and by the spring of 1922 it was becoming clear to the Board of the National Benzole Company that the whole future of benzole marketing was in jeopardy because they could not satisfy the demand they had created.

At this time, of course, National Benzole was still neat benzole, and the majority of motorists using benzole were using it neat. Many of them, however, were reverting to the pre-war practice of mixing it with petrol, especially those living or motoring in the remoter areas where National Benzole supplies were becoming inadequate. This habit, as before, led to a variety of engine performance, due partly to the poor quality of some of the petrol on the market and partly to the casual nature of the mixing. In fact, when blended scientifically, both petrol and benzole give better performance in combination than they do on their own. In one of the early trials in 1904, it will be remembered, it was found that benzole needed to be primed with petrol when starting from cold.

So the Company began to consider the possibility of marketing a benzole-petrol mixture. Such a scheme would enable them not only to control the mixture that went into the motorist's tank but also to spread the supplies of benzole over a far wider market. But it was not as easy as it sounds.

The research chemists in the benzole organisation would have to formulate a method of blending the two spirits, for it was more than a problem of merely mixing them together in a storage tank. Then, would all the depots be capable of carrying out the blending to an approved specification? How would the petrol be transported to the depots? Could the continuity of petrol supplies be assured?

All these problems would no doubt be solved, but the largest question mark was whether they would be able to get petrol supplies at all. Remember the Company had no connection with any petroleum producer, and it was not so easy to go cap in hand to the "oil men" to beg supplies of a high-grade petrol which, when mixed with Benzole was to be sold in competition with their own brands. The petrol firms naturally took full advantage of the Company's difficulty and renewed their efforts to buy them out. Tempting offers were made – and resisted.

However by forward-buying of petroleum cargoes while they were still on the high seas – a tricky operation, because the home market price might change before the tanker reached port – sufficient petrol stocks were built up to give the Company a start, and an ocean terminal for receiving the tankers was opened at Dingle, near Liverpool. A story is told that when the first ocean tanker arrived the local harbourmaster, unused to berthing tankers, and suddenly alarmed lest it should blow up and cause alarm and despondency amongst the inhabitants of Dingle, turned to the waiting N.B.C. engineer and said: "That's a petrol tanker, isn't it? I'm not sure I can allow it to berth here." The engineer said, "It's all right, it's for National Benzole." "Oh," said the harbourmaster, "it's benzole, is it? Well, of course that's different."

In July 1922 the plunge was taken, and the new National Benzole Mixture was launched, selling at a penny above the price of ordinary petrol. Both the benzole and the petrol were of a guaranteed quality, which was something quite new in the motor fuel business in those days, and motorists were not slow to respond. Backed by a lively publicity campaign, the new mixture got away to a splendid start.

At first the mixture contained benzole and petrol in equal quantities. "Fifty-fifty" was the great slogan in the press advertising, and "National 50-50" was what motorists asked for when filling up at garages even after the time when improvements in the refining techniques of both benzole and petrol made it possible to introduce

103

One of the first advertisements for National Benzole Mixture.

progressively more scientific and flexible blending formulae to keep pace with the steady advance in engine design.

By the autumn of 1922 benzole production had recovered from the coal strike, but the "Fifty-fifty" mixture was so successful that sales were outstripping the Company's petrol supply. Later in the same year, it is recorded, the Chairman and Directors paid a visit to America to "fix up petrol supplies", and a temporary arrangement was made with an American oil concern associated with the Agwi refinery at Fawley, near Southampton. In due course, however, a long-term contract for the supply of high-grade petrol was made with Anglo-Persian (now British Petroleum), thus establishing a supply arrangement which has continued unbroken ever since.

From 1923 onwards the Company could begin to draw breath and feel they were standing on solid ground. Already the offices in Grosvenor Gardens had become too small for the growing staff, and early that year the firm moved to Wellington House in Buckingham Gate, a spacious building which allowed for plenty of future expansion and was to be the Company's home for 36 years. The transport side of the business was growing up. Bulk deliveries had superseded the two-gallon can, and most of the original War Department lorries had been replaced by more up-to-date vehicles (with enclosed cabs now). The Company was, moreover, one of the first motor spirit concerns to introduce its own branded kerbside pumps into the garages.

Road deliveries had been supplemented by the inauguration of waterborne transport in the shape of a growing fleet of small coastal tankers, owned by the Company and carrying spirit by the more economical water routes from port to port around the coast of Britain. These were the well-known series of "Ben" Boats, all named after Directors of the Company. One of them, the *Ben Sadler*, which came into service in 1931, was the first self-propelled spirit barge allowed by the Port of London Authority to operate on the Thames; it had a double-skinned hull to comply with their safety regulations. These little tankers played their part later on in the Second World War, as we shall see.

Meanwhile, to return to the 'twenties, the Company's advertising had been losing no opportunity of ramming home the virtues of the new motor spirit. It is fascinating to run through the advertising files and follow the gradual change of style through the years, starting with the rather crude typographical layout of the early 'twenties and the assumption that the casual reader had plenty of time to read what you had to say. Here is some of the over-burdened "copy" from one of the first "Fifty-fifty" advertisements:

The Press has frequently remarked during the past weeks that motorists have no guarantee of quality when purchasing Motor Spirit. The purchaser is protected when buying National Benzole Mixture, for the quality is guaranteed. It is so skilfully blended that every drop that passes the carburettor proportionately ensures: 20% increased mileage, elimination of pinking. . . .

and so on. A more successful attempt to catch the fleeting eye was a graphic pictorial montage, with a petrol refinery on the one hand and a lurid, belching coke oven works on the other, and from each a stream of spirit flowing to join up together, under the words "Fifty-fifty", in the filler hole of a National Benzole Mixture 2-gallon can. Later comes a proud representation of the new petrol pump, surmounted with the slogan "The Holiday Spirit" – simple, neat and

It was a short step, after all, from "the Spirit with the Devil in it" to the athletic figure of Mr. Mercury.

effective. There was a good deal of play on the word "Spirit" – "The Spirit of the Future", "That's the Spirit" and so on, leading to the "The Spirit with the Devil in it", which caused such a furore amongst certain religious bodies that it had to be dropped. Constant search was going on all the time for a suitable trade-mark. At one period the jovial character of "Old King Coal" appeared in all the advertisements to remind motorists of benzole's carboniferous origin, but this idea was finally dropped in 1928 in favour of the brilliant conception of the winged "Mr Mercury", whose lithe, bronzed and startlingly naked figure was a considerable eye-catcher as it leapt across the pages of the national press.

In the same year the Company acquired the assets of the largest benzole distributor in the north, the Newcastle Benzol Company, who until then had retained their independence. By 1930 it could be said that 99% of the country's benzole production was at the disposal of the National Benzole Company. National Benzole Mixture was now well established as one of the four leading motor spirits in the country. "Mercury Head" pumps were to be seen everywhere. Exclusively National Benzole road-tankers were used for fuelling the army manœuvres of 1928. "Mr Mercury" was a popular subject with the Bright Young Things of those days at fancy dress balls, and he must surely be the only commercial trade mark that has ever inspired a fashion in ladies' hats!

When the German airship *Graf Zeppelin* visited England in 1930, National Benzole were able to make good propaganda for themselves out of the fact that her engines were running on a benzole-petrol mixture. This sombre photograph of the airship over London in April of that year is somehow reminiscent of the German air raids of the First World War. Was her visit as innocent as it seemed?

CHAPTER 9

The Years of Depression

1930-1939

By 1930 the post-war boom was over. In 1931 the Wall-Street "crash" set off a chain reaction of economic crises which affected the whole of America and Europe. There followed the inevitable sequence of depression which middle-aged readers will remember only too well – the industrial strife, the mounting unemployment, the "dole" queues, the bitterly resented Means Test, the 1936 march of unemployed from Jarrow to London, the Fascist and anti-Fascist rallies . . . and behind it all the looming, sinister shadow of Adolf Hitler. It was a miserable time, to be sure, and we ought to be glad we are not living in it now.

First to be affected by the economic slump were of course the high-performance luxury car and the expensive sports car. Rolls-Royce and Daimler were well established and in a class of their own, but many famous concerns, including Bentley, Lanchester and Sunbeam, were swallowed up or went out of business during the 1930's. Others managed to survive by turning their attention to the mass-production of smaller and duller cars.

Unfortunately automobile design was entering into the worst decade of its whole history. The new mass-production technique was in its infancy, and the designers had not yet mastered its problems. Gone for the most part was the natural unpretentious grace that distinguished the Vintage car and came from a basis of sound engineering principle and fitness for purpose. Cars now began to be designed for effect, and to suit the current convenience of assembly-line production.

Moreover, the uncertain economic conditions of the time sharpened the edge of competition (in 1932 Morris marketed a £100 car!) and gave the Sales Department a stronger hand at the conference table. The great majority of the new motoring public, for whom the assembly lines were churning out their thousands of vehicles, had no conception or experience of the finer points of driving. All they wanted was a car that would seat the family and the dog in not too much discomfort and take them out for a run at the weekends to look at the countryside. They had no interest in road-holding, gear-ratios, brake horse-power or other technical matters. As long as the car had four wheels, an engine under the bonnet, a roof to keep the rain out and a decent bit of chromium at the front to make it look smart, they were fairly satisfied. So the Sales Department demanded a low price, more room for the passengers, more gadgets and an exterior that would impress the neighbours. These requirements could only be met by sacrificing some of the precepts of sound engineering design. The engine was gradually moved farther forward, the back-seat passengers farther back, the wheelbase was shortened – with the result that weight was coming more and more over the axles and so reducing the stability of the car. Many of the popular family saloons of this period were positively unsafe, a menace to the owners themselves and everybody else on the roads. And the steadily increasing overall weight was making many once excellent models much too heavy for the power of the engine.

Some of these defects naturally affected the road-holding and performance of many of the cheap sports cars which began to be very popular in the early part of the 'thirties, for these were in fact mostly based on a mass-production chassis with a slightly hotted up engine and an eye-catching, sporty body (and if the bonnet had a thick strap round it and a chromium-plated exhaust-pipe curving away from it along the side of the car, so much the better!). But they provided an enormous amount of fun for thousands who could not afford a Sunbeam or a Bentley, and some of them, like the Wolseley Hornets, the Morgans (which had three wheels until 1936), the "Le Mans" Singer Nines, the Triumphs, the Austin Sevens,

Singer 9-h.p. "Le Mans" sports
car of 1935.

were genuine cars and performed prodigious deeds in countless
competitive events at Brooklands and elsewhere. A Triumph
Gloria driven by Donald Healey won the light-car class in the Monte
Carlo Rally of 1934. Special mention should be made of the M.G.
Midget. The first M.G. was constructed in 1923 by Cecil Kimber
out of Morris parts (including the Cowley "bull nose"); with

The first M.G. of 1923

An M.G. "T.A." Midget of 1936, of which even unsupercharged versions lapped Brooklands at over 90 m.p.h.

Morris's blessing it developed into one of the most popular small sports cars of all time, and under Kimber's direction had a great run of racing successes. The Midget was built almost entirely of Morris Minor components, underwent several variations, and developed into the 1936 PB type which, when supercharged, was capable of 100 m.p.h. and was perhaps the finest small production sports car ever made.

More affluent sportsmen, lucky enough not to be affected too seriously by the sad state of the share market, had quite a wide

A Rolls-Royce Phantom II with the "Continental" short chassis, about 1932

Dignified, powerful, and unmistakably English. A Rolls-Royce
Phantom III sports limousine with Mulliner body.

selection of fast, comfortable cars to choose from. Heading the list
was the "Continental" version of the Rolls-Royce Phantom II, to
be superseded in the mid 'thirties by the first twelve-cylinder Rolls –
the Phantom III – one of which ghosted all the way from Derby
to Nairobi and back with no sign of any mechanical trouble whatso-
ever, without even the addition of a single drop of water to the
radiator.

Slightly more sporting in appearance, though unable to match
the Rolls for dignity, was the new Hispano-Suiza. It will be
remembered how the great $6\frac{1}{2}$-litre made a sensational debut at
the opening of the Vintage Era in 1919. The same firm now made
their not inconsiderable mark at the beginning of the post-Vintage
decade with another fabulous car, so expensive (the chassis price

alone was £3,000) that very few can have been sold in Great Britain at that time. This was the 9½-litre V-12, in which the stroke was exactly equal to the bore, 100 millimetres each. It was a 100 m.p.h. machine of the utmost luxury and silence, the only other car in the world that could be said to rival the Phantom III – which it preceded by four years.

Rolls-Royce had presumably bought the Bentley name for very good reasons, and the motoring world waited with interest to see what they would do with it. The answer came at the Motor Show in 1933, when the prototype of the 3½-litre Bentley was shown, with

The first of the Rolls-Royce Bentleys, with Woolf Barnato at the wheel. It was marketed under the slogan, "The Silent Sports Car".

a hotted-up Rolls-Royce 25 h.p. engine and a sleeker Bentley exterior complete with the familiar winged-B radiator. W. O. Bentley, retained by Rolls on a service contract, had contributed a good deal to the design, and though Bentley enthusiasts were disappointed

that it was not more specifically a sports car, the result was certainly
a very high-performance touring car of delightful appearance,
bearing strong traces of the old Bentley "sportiness" and yet characterised by the Rolls smoothness, silence and superb finish. Moreover
it had a four-speed synchromesh gearbox and the Rolls-Royce
servo-assisted brakes, and has turned out to be one of the most
durable sports cars ever produced. In 1936 the engine was enlarged
to $4\frac{1}{4}$-litres, giving a top speed of 95 m.p.h.

At the end of his contract with Rolls, Bentley became technical
director of the reconstructed Lagonda firm. The $4\frac{1}{2}$-litre Lagonda
had just taken first place in the 1935 Le Mans, and Bentley set
about making refinements to this car which both made it quieter
and enabled it to do well over 90 m.p.h. with no trouble at all.
In 1937 came "W.O.'s" last masterpiece, the Lagonda V-12,

The Bentley-designed Lagonda V-12

with an unusually short-stroke engine which produced effortless smoothness and flexibility. The firm decided to enter two cars for the 1939 Le Mans – at rather short notice, so much so that one of the cars had its first road test on the way to Newhaven to catch the cross-Channel boat. The two cars, under orders to keep down to an average of 83 m.p.h., had trouble-free runs and took third and fourth places.

The war broke out a week or so later and further development on this remarkable car had to come to a full stop. After the war Lagonda built the prototype of a Bentley-designed 2½-litre, but before it could be put into production the firm was sold up, the prototype and the engine design being bought by the David Brown organisation, who put the 2½ Lagonda on the market pretty well as it was, and concurrently developed the engine as the power unit for the D.B. Aston Martin.

Though W. O. Bentley himself is no longer actively associated with car manufacture, it must be a source of great satisfaction to this great designer, who has done so much for British reputation in car sport and motor engineering, to know that his name is already a legend and that his brain-children and their descendants are still in the fore-front of the sports car world.

A recent photograph of W. O., who must have known as much contrast of triumph and misfortune as anyone else in the motor business. His recent autobiography made entertaining reading, and was described by one reviewer as "a book for every man who drove a green Bentley through a daydream to win a woman or Le Mans".

Invicta was another promising large sports car which, like the Bentley, was dragged down by the undertow of the slump. The indefatigable Miss Violet Cordery had driven the first model, the 1925 3-litre, round the world to win the Dewar Trophy for 1927, and (with her sister as co-driver) won it again the following year by driving the new 4½-litre 30,000 miles at an average speed of 60 m.p.h. – a remarkable feat of endurance. The 4½ was then developed by Donald Healey into a "100 m.p.h." car with improved

A 1931 4½-litre "100-m.p.h." Invicta.

road-holding qualities, and with this car he won the Monte Carlo Rally of 1931, the second British victory in the history of the event – the first having been the 1925 victory of the Hon. and Mrs. Victor Bruce driving an A.C. It was a great pity that Invicta production had to cease in 1934.

The collapse of the Sunbeam-Talbot–Darracq combine in 1935 has been related in an earlier chapter. That it lasted as long as it did was due not only to the unspent impetus of Sunbeam's glorious years, but also to the increasing racing successes of the Roesch-designed Talbots, especially in the opening years of the 1930's. Whereas it had been the Sunbeams which took the weight in the 1920's, it was now the turn of the Talbots to carry the burden of the dying business. When Bentley won his last Le Mans in 1930, third and fourth places were taken by Talbot "90's", cars of only 2276 ccs., or one-third the capacity of the Bentleys, which were 6½-litre. Talbots were in fact the only British cars making any kind of impression in racing during these rather lean years, and it was a sad day when they were pulled down by the Sunbeam collapse and the break-up of the S.T.D. combine. Like Sunbeams, Talbots then came under the Rootes wing and played no further part in the racing field.

In fact, with the Sunbeam decline in the later Vintage years, Britain now had no car that could put up any serious opposition in international Grand Prix racing. The outlook was dismal in the extreme. Even France, represented by Bugatti, fell gradually behind in the struggle to compete with first Italy and then Germany, both of whom had the full weight and support of their authoritarian régimes behind them. The first three or four years of the decade were dominated by the Alfa-Romeos, especially the "monoposto" P.3 driven by Tazio Nuvolari, whom many consider to be the

The sweets of victory. Tazio Nuvolari after the 1933 Ulster T.T.

Rudolf Caracciola, the brilliant pre-war Mercedes driver, who won seventeen races during 1934-1939.

greatest racing driver who has ever lived. In 1934 (the year after Hitler's accession to power) Germany re-entered Grand Prix racing, and the remaining years of "peace" developed into a rivalry between two German teams: Mercedes, led by Rudolf Caracciola, the other great driver of this period, and Auto-Union – with other countries nowhere. Only Alfa-Romeo were able to make any kind of show at all, their best moment being in 1935 when they infuriated Hitler by winning the German Grand Prix at Nürburgring and defeating the much-propaganda-ed new German cars. The famous British driver Richard Seaman was one of the Mercedes driving team during their years of dominance, and in this capacity became the third British driver ever to win a *grand épreuve*. (The second British driver to achieve this was the French-domiciled Williams, who drove a Bugatti to win the 1929 Monaco Grand Prix. The first, Segrave, was the only one to date who had done so in a British car, with his Sunbeam victories in the 1923 French Grand Prix and the 1924 Spanish Grand Prix.)

Nazi Germany's all-conquering participation in Grand Prix racing was no mere propaganda move. The experience gained in it was made full use of in the development of fighter aero-engines.

119

We must be thankful for Rolls-Royce and their Merlin engines –
and for Lady Houston, who sponsored the Vickers-Supermarine
racing seaplanes which used them!

In the medium-priced sports car range a dwindling number of
British manufacturers strove gallantly to uphold the Vintage
traditions which they themselves had helped to establish. The still
chain-driven Frazer Nash, the A.C. with the same Weller engine

The chain drive of a 1927 "Boulogne" Frazer Nash. Instantaneous
gear-change was effected through sliding dog clutches on the cross-
shaft to the left of the picture. Gear ratios could be fairly easily altered
to suit the customer's taste.

design dating back to 1919 (and so good that it has lasted well on into the 1950's!), the Rover, the Riley, the Alvis, the Bertelli-designed Aston Martin – these and a few others kept the flag flying despite the economic slump. On the other side of the Channel, and rather more expensive, were Bugatti, Delage, Delahaye, Darracq (post-S.T.D.), Hotchkiss (almost habitual winner of the Monte Carlo Rally) – all struggling to survive in a contracting

Frazer Nash refinement. The twin-o.h.c. 6-cylinder Blackburne engine fitted from 1933 to 1936, with a single-camshaft Gough as an alternative. These engines replaced the Meadows engine of the early 'thirties which had superseded the famous side-valve Anzani engine.

121

sports car market. In Italy the Alfa-Romeos were still supreme in the luxury market, and lower down the financial scale the Fiats and the Lancias were still to the fore. In Germany Mercedes-Benz concentrated on their Grand Prix racing *blitzkrieg* but on the commercial side were satisfied, like most other German manufacturers at this time, with a series of rather large, humdrum cars.

During the post-Vintage decade two promising newcomers began to take a hand in the sports car game – one in Britain and one in Germany. A Blackpool firm of specialist bodywork makers called SS Cars Ltd. first attracted serious attention in the early 'thirties with their Swallow Special, based on a 16 h.p. Standard chassis. This developed gradually into a very attractive and beautifully made open sports car. In 1935 Mr Lyons marketed the $2\frac{1}{2}$-litre SS. 90, first of the "Jaguar" series, designed by W. M. Heynes, and three years later followed it with the famous push-rod $3\frac{1}{2}$-litre Jaguar SS. 100. These Jaguars were a portent for the future, forerunners of the wonderfully successful and comparatively inexpensive sports cars (all with twin overhead-camshaft engines) which the firm, now re-formed as Jaguar Cars Ltd., have poured forth from their

The forefather of the Jaguar: the 6-cylinder SS 1 of 1931, the first car ever made by SS Cars Ltd (now Jaguar Cars Ltd).

123

The rakish lines of the 1938 Jaguar SS. 100

Coventry factory since the war, to the great benefit of British prestige abroad.

The new German entry in the field was B.M.W., who started life by manufacturing Austin Sevens under licence. In 1932, under the inspiration of their new designer Dr Fritz Fiedler, they began producing a six-cylinder tourer, enlarged the engine capacity slightly to make it a $1\frac{1}{2}$-litre and turned it into a sports car. This did so well in the 1933 Alpine Trials that Frazer Nash immediately acquired the English rights. The Frazer Nash B.M.W. of 1936, the 2-litre Type 328 "Grand Prix" model, was a fast, lithe, versatile two-seater sports tourer which perhaps represents the peak of pre-war small sports car design.

The outlook for British racing cars and sports cars did not seem too promising by 1939. However, British drivers and British cars continued successfully to attack and improve on the world land speed record which, it will be remembered, Henry Segrave had established in 1930 at 231.446 m.p.h. First to make the attempt after Lee Bible had been killed in the White-Triplex was the well-known Brooklands racing driver Kaye Don, but his specially built 4½-ton twin-engined Sunbeam "Silver Bullet" proved to be less powerful than expected and failed even to reach the double century. The indomitable Malcolm Campbell, after a frustrating and unsuccessful attempt in his rebuilt "Bluebird" on a dried-up lake-

First at 250 and 300 m.p.h., Sir Malcolm Campbell

bed at Verneuk in South Africa, then fitted his car with a 1450 h.p. Napier aero engine and took it once again to Daytona, where in January 1931 he broke the record with 246 m.p.h. Like Segrave, he was knighted on his return to England. A year later he passed another coveted landmark by pushing his own record up to 254 m.p.h.

Campbell now determined to reach the next round figure of 300 m.p.h. With the latest Rolls-Royce aero engine providing 2,500 horse-power under "Bluebird's" bonnet he persistently improved on his own figure – 272 m.p.h. in 1933, 276 in 1935 – until finally in a big jump later the same year he succeeded in achieving 301 m.p.h. on Bonneville Salt Flats at Utah, near Salt Lake City. Content to go down in history as the first man to pass the 300 mark, he decided to leave it at that and devote his attention

Sir Malcolm Campbell with "Bluebird", photographed in 1933 shortly before his successful attempt to beat his own record then standing at 254 m.p.h. With him is his son Donald, present holder of the world water speed record.

to attacking the water speed record – in which, too, he was successful.

Surely, it was said again, the limit had now been reached? Two other familiar figures on Brooklands track, George Eyston and John Cobb, did not think so. Eyston, putting his faith in size and brute force, built a special car powered by two Rolls-Royce aero engines giving a total of 5,000 horse-power. The "Thunderbolt" weighed six tons, and was the heaviest and most powerful car ever made. With this monster Eyston raised the record to 312 in 1937 and again to 345 in 1938. But he was foiled in his ambition to be the first to reach 350 m.p.h., for John Cobb took the record at 350 m.p.h. a week or so

The present world land speed record-holder, the late John Cobb.

later, driving a car only half the weight and with only half the power – a Napier-engined record-breaker designed by Reid Railton – and incidentally for this occasion using a special benzole mixture prepared for him by the National Benzole Company's research department. However, twenty-four hours later Eyston leap-frogged Cobb with 357 m.p.h. Not to be outdone, the following year Cobb went back to Utah and clocked 369.74 m.p.h., and there the record stood at the outbreak of war.

After the war, in 1947, Cobb made a brave attempt to hoist the record up to the coveted 400, but although on his first run he actually averaged 403 m.p.h., the mean average of the two runs was 394.16 m.p.h. Cobb, too, then succumbed to the lure of travelling fast on water. Like Segrave before him, this outstanding driver was killed when, in 1952, his jet-propelled speedboat "Crusader" somersaulted and sank during an attempt to break the world water speed record on Loch Ness. But his world land speed record has remained unbeaten to this day, though with the development of the gas turbine engine it is not likely to do so for long.

By 1939 the manufacturing standards and the design of the "ordinary" car were just beginning their long climb out of the abyss into which they had fallen in the early 1930's. The designers were at last learning how to master the new mass production techniques instead of being enslaved by them. Some of the improvement must also be credited to the persistent influence of the large number of enthusiasts who, by forming themselves into such organisations as the Vintage Sports Car Club (founded in 1934), sought to preserve the old Vintage conception of what a car should be. At any rate, whatever the causes, towards the end of this somewhat depressing decade there were budding signs of an all-round improvement. Unfortunately we had to wait until the war and its aftermath had subsided before it was able to come to fruition.

On facing page:

Above: John Cobb in the cockpit of the 2,500-h.p. Railton-designed special in which he set up the present world land speed record. This attempt was sponsored by an American oil concern, but the car was all-British, being built by a Brooklands engineering firm.

Below: The memory of Vintage marques has also been kept alive by the sports car owners who banded themselves into clubs like the Bentley Drivers Club, the Aston Martin Owners Club, the Lagonda Car Club, and so on. Here is an attack on Nailsworth Ladder by the Bugatti Owners Club.

CHAPTER 10

Mr Mercury Spreads His Wings

Whether they were well designed or not, the thousands of cars that were rolling off the assembly lines all needed fuel. The sales of National Benzole Mixture, which had been further stimulated in 1929 by a reduction to 1s. 5d. a gallon, bringing it level with the price of petrol, continued to increase steadily and only ten years after opening their first tiny office in 1919 the erstwhile "pirates" of Horseferry Road found themselves well up amongst the leading motor spirit concerns. During the 1930's, despite the slump and the uneconomic "price war" which prevailed for a time during the most acute period of the depression, the National Benzole Company proceeded to consolidate the position they had fought for, both by further development of the distributing organisation and by enterprising forms of publicity.

They were the first motor spirit company to introduce large posters to the hoardings, employing top-ranking commercial artists like Tom Purvis, and there is no doubt that the 16- and 48-sheet posters showing Mercury speeding on winged feet through the darkness towards a sunrise horizon, or beckoning the motorist past the next milestone, or reaching across the dashboard to press the starter button and give point to the newly coined word "start-ability" were brilliantly conceived. Later in the period came the ingenious slogan, "Oh Mr Mercury, you did give me a start" – which gave motorists a bit of a start, too, when the pretty girl in the driving seat, with Mr Mercury sitting boldly beside her, distracted their attention as they drove along the new, and as yet un-built-up, arterial roads. National Benzole were also the first fuel concern to make a documentary film about their product, the first to introduce aluminium road tankers to this country, and the first to operate

an aircraft refuelling service station – at Croydon (when Croydon was London's airport).

The Company's interest in aviation was further signalised by the purchase of a Puss Moth aircraft and the appointment of their Manchester Representative, Mr J. J. Scholes, as pilot and Aviation Representative. Painted the National Benzole chrome yellow and black, and with the winged-head trade mark on the rudder, it was christened "Mercury I" by Mrs Henshaw, the wife of the Chairman, at a ceremony at Castle Bromwich on May 11th 1931. "Mercury I" was followed by others, and these planes caused no little stir by appearing regularly at aviation events up and down the country. Many of the competitors at these events were using National Benzole Mixture in their aircraft, and in 1934 no less than seven of the major air events of the year were won on it. The National Benzole aviation refuelling tankers, made at the Company's own workshops in Willesden, were the first of their kind to appear on British aerodromes. It was the only spirit employed by Sir Alan Cobham's annual touring Air Circus for several years, and it provided the fuel for many of the entries in the annual King's Cup Air Race, finding the winner in 1932 and 1935 and the runner-up in 1931 and 1934. The fact that on all these occasions the mixture was the same standard National Benzole Mixture that any motorist could buy from the pump was proof of its performance value for all types of internal combustion engine, and

131

National Benzole tankers fuelling aircraft during the 1930's

every opportunity was taken of underlining this fact in the firm's press advertising.

Perhaps the greatest boost of all came from the Company's association with John Cobb in his long series of record-breaking achievements at Brooklands and elsewhere. Driving his famous Napier-Railton Special, and using guaranteed pump-standard National Benzole Mixture, he won innumerable races and record titles. Finally in 1935 he established the ultimate Brooklands lap record of 143.44 m.p.h. – which on that constricted circuit must have been a somewhat hair-raising experience.

In April 1934 Cobb took the car to Montlhéry, the well-known racing track just outside Paris, to make an attempt on the world 24-hour record. Unfortunately appalling weather robbed him and his team of drivers of their chief prize. Torrential rainstorms made a river of the track, and after driving heroically for nearly twenty hours they were obliged to abandon the attempt when the car skidded off the track at nearly 130 m.p.h. They had, however, established five new world records, including the 12-hour record at an average of 121 m.p.h.

Undaunted by this partial failure Cobb decided to make a further

John Cobb with the Napier-Railton Special, about to make one of his
record attempts at Brooklands.

attempt in 1935 – not at Montlhéry but on the wide open spaces
on the Bonneville salt flats at Utah, where presently he was
to make the successful attacks on the world land speed record
already recounted. This time he and his co-drivers were entirely
successful, taking the world 6-, 12- and 24-hour records at a final
average of 134.7 m.p.h. In the following year they raised them
all again, covering 3,600 miles at an average of 150 m.p.h.

Standard grade National Benzole Mixture was used in these
achievements. For the Utah record runs supplies were shipped by
the Company to America, and to prove there were no special in-
gredients in the fuel supplied, arrangements were made for the
Automobile Association of America to take samples of it and send
them to London. There they were examined by a well-known firm
of analysts and compared with samples taken at random by *Autocar*
representatives from National Benzole pumps. The result of the
analysis was published in the *Autocar*, which reported that "in the
opinion of the analysts all the samples can be considered identical
within the usual commercial limits, and to be equal in quality".

133

For his 1936 attack on the world 24-hour record at Utah Cobb used National Benzole Mixture which had been left over from the previous year and kept in sealed storage. That he was able to do so and still surpass his earlier record was a tribute to the "inhibiting" process which had been invented and developed in the Willesden research laboratories of the National Benzole Company by W. H. Hoffert and G. Claxton. This process stabilises the quality of motor spirit and prevents it from "resinification", or gumming-up, when it is stored for long periods. Originally developed with special reference to benzole, the process can be applied, with suitable modifications, to all forms of motor spirit. Made available not only to the benzole refineries but to the whole of the petroleum industry, it has revolutionised the motor spirit storage problem.

In the early 'twenties the National Benzole Company had set up a "control" laboratory at their headquarters in Wellington House. The control chemists' duties included regular testing of all competitive spirits, routine analysis of both the petrol and the benzole delivered to the depots for blending as National Benzole Mixture, and sample checks of the resultant mixtures to ensure that they were up to specification. At the same time benzole research was carried on at Leeds University in co-operation with the National Benzole Association and the results were published annually for the benefit of the benzole industry.

This dual arrangement led to considerable overlapping, and in 1930 the research chemists from Leeds joined the control chemists from Wellington House in new splendidly equipped laboratories under one roof at Willesden. Adjoining the laboratories was an engine testing section containing experimental apparatus for testing power output and fuel consumption, starting characteristics, freezing and vaporising points, and means of reproducing in a few hours the effects of several months' normal depot storage. The department also housed specially constructed engines for observing the behaviour and efficiency of motor spirits under operating conditions. These included the Ricardo engine used for determining the "anti-knock" value of spirits in terms of what was then known as the H.U.C.R., or "highest useful compression ratio". Ricardo's machine was later superseded by the C.F.R. engine, a single-cylinder unit in which the degree of knock can be experimentally varied by adjusting the compression ratio while the engine is running. Anti-knock value is now calibrated in terms of a standard "octane-number" scale. A low-octane spirit when ignited under high compression will explode, producing "knock", instead of burning smoothly through the combustion chamber. The more efficient high-compression engine of the modern car needs a spirit with a greater resistance to "knock", hence the higher-octane "super" blends of spirit available today. But the "super" petrol of today was only in its research stage during the 1930's.

In 1931 Hoffert and Claxton made a notable contribution to the scientific study of the aromatic hydrocarbons by publishing the first edition of their great technical work, *Motor Benzole, Its Production and Use*, soon recognised throughout the industry as the standard work on the subject.

The advertising word "startability", used to such good effect during the 1930's, was inspired by an entirely "unsolicited testimonial" which appeared in 1933. Professor W. A. Whatmough, a well-known motor engineer, contributed to the *Automobile Engineer* an article entitled "The Startability of Motor Fuels", in which he analysed the starting-up characteristics of four leading motor spirits. His conclusion was unequivocal: "National Benzole Mixture, the progenitor of petrols enriched with aromatics, presents the paradox of high gravity and extra poundage per gallon combined with extraordinary volatility . . . Judged upon its all-in average, it ranks as the easiest starting motor spirit. The exceptional starting-up properties of National Benzole Mixture are undoubtedly due to the additional vaporisability conferred upon the blend by the high proportion of benzole peculiar to this fuel."

Imagine how the advertising department went to town on that!

Meanwhile the salesmen were "going to town" all over Britain. New depots were being established every year and the road tanker fleet had developed into one of the most efficient and up to date commercial fleets in the country. Occasionally even an efficient modern tanker can have its moments of mishap, however, and in this connection Mr G. W. Downing, foreman of the Grimsby depot, tells an amusing story:

The most exciting moment we have had at the depot was sometime before the war, when a chap on a cycle rushed into the depot and told us that one of our tankers was on fire in the main street of Grimsby. It was driver Elliott with 1,500 gallons of National Benzole Mixture on board. The representative's car was in the depot and I got hold of our depot fire extinguisher and dashed about a quarter of a mile to where our tanker was and helped to put the fire out.

Of course, a great crowd had collected by this time, and the house opposite was in a state of excitement as the daughter was getting married that morning. Her mother shouted upstairs, "Mary, you had better hurry up if you want to get married. There's a Benzole lorry outside on fire and may blow up any minute," which caused a great laugh amongst the crowd.

The depots had come a long way since the early days, and the primitive conditions of some of the first make-shift premises were by now a fading memory. The Nottingham depot, however, had a difficult time when in May 1932 the River Trent rose to an unprecedented level and overflowed its banks. Mr R. H. Flint, the depot foreman, remembers how

All roads approaching the depot were under water. The river had surrounded the storage tanks and entered the pump house. On this morning one driver volunteered to wade down the road in high boots, got out his vehicle and drove it to where the staff were waiting to get down to the depot. It was between two open fields, and as it was all under water he had to guess where the road was. Fortunately his sense of direction was good and the staff by standing on the hose racks were delivered to the depot. In spite of the conditions deliveries did not cease. A brass plate recording the water-level was erected and is still in position in the pump house.

By the middle of the 'thirties National Benzole had the bit between their teeth. As one of the northern Divisions reported, "sales continue to expand at an alarming rate." This "alarming" but no doubt satisfactory expansion continued despite the sharpening world tension caused by Hitler's arrogant demands.

In September 1938 at the height of the "Munich" crisis, the Government proclaimed a state of national emergency. An embargo was placed on the sale of motor spirit in cans to prevent hoarding, the price of spirit was frozen at its current level, and the principals of the four leading spirit distributors – Shell-Mex and B.P. Ltd, the Anglo-American Oil Company Ltd, Trinidad Leaseholds Ltd and The National Benzole Company Ltd – were asked to formulate a plan for co-ordinating the country's oil distribution on a war basis. Together they set up the Petroleum Board. It must have been a proud moment for Mr Hittinger (who had been appointed Managing Director of National Benzole in the previous year) when he walked into the first meeting of the Petroleum Board to represent his company. Not so long ago he had been sitting in that small office in the Horseferry Road, sole accountant of a new business that still had to make its way in the motor fuel world.

The Petroleum Board met almost daily at this time to examine the countless problems of a scheme designed to come into immediate operation in the event of an outbreak of war. Although the Munich "Agreement" caused a temporary easing of the tension, few responsible men imagined it afforded anything but a breathing-space, and the work of preparation went on. During the autumn of 1938 the Board set up committees to work out detailed emergency arrangements for the pooling of material resources and technicians, the participation of the smaller oil industries, the special problems of fire-fighting and A.R.P. in spirit storage depots, and to make recommendations for a drastic reduction in the number of grades of petroleum products.

The formation and operation of the Petroleum Board, under its Chairman, Sir Andrew Agnew, was a striking instance of enlightened Government policy and the resilience of the democratic way of life. It was not a statutory body, and its work depended not on any rigid agreement with the Government but on the kind of day-to-day personal contacts by which business is normally run and which alone could achieve flexibility in meeting the variable requirements of the war machine. It was to be an executive body working under the general direction of the Government, and the job of supplying the petroleum needs of the forces and of war industry was to be left to men who were accustomed to such operations. The Government said what it wanted; the oil industry, through the Petroleum Board, was allowed to get on with it in its own way.

The need for secrecy in the early stages precluded the training of staff and meant that all planning had to be done on paper. The Pool scheme was based on a series of agreements between the thirty-six companies involved, who between them contracted in the event of war to place at the Board's disposal physical assets and capital totalling about fifty million pounds. Remuneration, on terms authorised by the Government, was to be distributed to the members of the Board on a proportional basis calculated partly on their financial and physical contribution and partly on their 1938 turnover. The agreements also laid down the conditions for a return to a fully competitive industry after the war.

During the war an American oil expert made a survey of the way Britain had organised her oil industry for the emergency, and reported as follows:

> The oil men of Great Britain have fashioned an effective "monopoly" of oil for the purpose of prosecuting the war, but they have also, they feel sure, arranged to ensure the return of a truly free and competitive oil industry when the war is concluded.
>
> Perhaps the most striking feature of this "monopolistic" arrangement is the informal way in which the legal side has been handled, not only as between the oil men but with their government. Over in the U.S. it is certain any such arrangements would be hedged about with a multitude of opinions, probably court decisions, a few acts of Congress, and the whole continually scrutinised, undoubtedly with some suspicion, by many government departments and agencies with frequent voicing of criticism, especially by those least informed.
>
> And at the end it is not improbable that every oil man party to such a war "monopoly" might have to stand trial, at least in test cases, to see if he had violated his country's alleged laws even to win the war.

The skill and imagination of the men who carried through the Petroleum Board's vast financial merger has never been widely enough recognised. It was the speediest, the most boldly conceived and the most dramatic operation of its kind ever undertaken, and the Pool was in action from the very moment when, on September 3rd 1939, Neville Chamberlain broadcast to the nation the news that Great Britain had declared war on Germany.

It was to be over thirteen years before National Benzole Mixture could be sold under its own name again.

CHAPTER 11

Dealing with Hitler & Co.

1939-1945

Zero hour for the great oil merger was fixed for midnight of the same day, Sunday September 3rd. When the staff of the National Benzole Company arrived for work on the following morning they found, like the staff of all the motor spirit companies, that overnight and without warning (for the plans had been kept secret) they had become employees of the Petroleum Board. In many cases they had to take up unaccustomed duties under strange bosses and it must have been odd at first to be working in co-operation with new colleagues who, up to the previous Saturday, had been fierce competitors.

Every office and depot had *ipso facto* become a Petroleum Board establishment. National Benzole Mixture, the sales of which that year had been at their highest to date, disappeared into the common "pool". The lorry drivers looked on with dismay as their proud road-tankers lost their distinctive chrome yellow under a drab coat of grey paint. The sales departments of the company's divisional offices all over the country had to shed their competitive instincts and meanwhile cope with the rush of orders as the public, contrary to regulations, tried to stock up before rationing should begin. Motorists queued at garages as soon as word got round that a "pool" tanker had been making a delivery. Thousands of normally honest citizens bought as much petrol as they could carry away, storing it in cans, pails, dustbins, jars, bottles – any kind of container, with or without lid, that didn't have a hole in the bottom.

Two respectable maiden ladies of Beckenham had the embarrassing experience of being run in when the police discovered a considerable quantity of spirit dangerously concealed in their attic bedroom in basins and hip baths.

Three weeks after the outbreak of war petrol rationing came into force and put a stop to the hoarding scramble, though it could not entirely prevent the inevitable "smart operator" from diverting into the black market a small proportion of the oil cargoes which merchant seamen were risking their lives to bring across thousands of miles of ocean.

The Petroleum Board had no rationing powers of its own, but it could only supply spirit against the appropriate value of coupons, and large staffs had to be kept busy checking the parcels of coupons which accompanied orders from retailers. By the end of the war the Petroleum Board's turnover amounted to an average of a million pounds each working day, calling for a tremendous volume of

The wartime shortage of petrol led to the widespread use of gas as a motor fuel. Here is Mr. Geoffrey Lloyd, then Secretary for Mines, inspecting one of the new gas-producing trailers in November 1939. Many private motorists drove with unwieldy-looking gas-bags on the roofs of their cars.

accounting and book-keeping to keep track of storage, sales, supplies, tanker freights, insurance, the acquisition and receiving of stocks from overseas, and transactions with the Government over Lend-Lease supplies from America.

Many deeds of valour were performed during the air raids by members of the Petroleum Board's staff, by the firefighters of the storage depots, by the clerical workers in the badly blitzed towns, by the drivers of the road tankers. Thanks to their efforts, inspired perhaps by the competitive attitude bred in times of peace – that "deliveries must go on" – petroleum supplies were never seriously held up at any time throughout the war, and during the invasion operations from D-Day onwards not a single ship was delayed in sailing for want of fuel.

Into all this gigantic work the National Benzole Company threw the whole of its weight. Meanwhile their "Ben" Boats were running the gauntlet in the dangerous convoys up the swept channels through the East Coast minefields, harried by E-boats and Focke-Wulfs. The *Ben Robinson* acted as a water-boat for our troops at Arromanches, going over on D-Day and remaining there until she was no longer required. One "Ben" Boat only was lost – the *Ben Hann*, a brand new vessel which was sunk with all hands off the Mull of Kintyre in November 1941.

Soon after the outbreak of war the majority of the staff at Wellington House were evacuated to a country mansion at Stonor Park in Oxfordshire. For those who had to remain in London the whole of the basement, which normally housed the staff recreation club, was converted into an air raid shelter. Wellington House came through the blitz virtually unscathed, but the new research laboratories at Willesden were completely gutted by incendiary bombs.

As in the first world war, benzole was again required in large quantities for the manufacture of explosives, and again many new benzole-producing plants were erected to meet the demand, raising the annual home production of benzole by many millions of gallons.

The sleeker trend in post-war body-styling. The Ford Zephyr, seen here in its attractive convertible version, was one of the first of the new-style family cars of the early 1950's which made a notable advance on their pre-war counterparts. Its 2¼-litre, 6-cylinder, overhead-valve engine provided lively performance on the new premier grades of spirit which came on the market when Pool spirit was finally abandoned in 1953.

CHAPTER 12

Motoring Since the War

1945-1959

As the six-year struggle came to its sourly triumphant end the ordinary man in the street put aside his uniform, got the old car out of the garage and looked forward to a return to peaceable mobility. The car manufacturers again set about beating their swords into ploughshares; from the production lines which had for so long been disgorging tanks, armoured cars, aero-engines and other war machines, private cars once more began to roll – and they were soon to roll forth in such quantities that driving on English roads on high days and holidays was to become something of a procession.

On the other hand, the standards of design and performance were presently to show a marked improvement on those of the pre-war years. Not at once, however. It will be remembered that at the Motor Show in 1919, less than a year after the end of the First World War, several exciting new designs were ready to be shown to the public, either in production or as prototypes. After the Second World War it was considerably longer before new models began to appear on the home market. This was due to a variety of causes.

Most cars are now mass-produced, and it takes a year or two even to "tool up" for a new mass-production design; until 1946, moreover, the car factories had been engaged on war work. There was also an acute shortage of steel. Manufacturers saw no point in laying out large sums in tooling up for a new design if they were not going to be allowed enough steel to produce it in sufficient quantities to make it an economic proposition. Another factor was the uncertainty of the motor spirit situation. Rationing, it is true, was abolished in 1950, but Pool Spirit remained until 1953; and though manufacturers were already working on designs for higher compression engines, it was no use giving higher compression to the motorist unless he could get higher octane spirit from the filling stations. Manufacturers therefore tended to hold back on the production of new models until they could turn over to higher compression engines. Meanwhile there was no difficulty in selling all the cars they could make on the pre-war patterns. For six years motorists had been unable to replace their old cars, and during the interregnum a new generation of would-be motorists had grown up. Too many people were wanting too few cars. Because of the long waiting lists for new cars, second-hand prices rose to ridiculous figures – often well above the list price of a new car of the same model.

For a while, then, the British motorist had to be content with a pre-war second-hand car or, if he was lucky, a new car that was still basically of pre-war design. A year or two after the war, how-ever, he began to see the occasional new American car parked in London, attracting a small crowd with its unusually large window area, its low, full-chassis-width bonnet and boot, and its pastel colouring. Of course, you couldn't tell front from back, it was a glasshouse on wheels, it was showy – and the colours were really a bit too much. So most of us thought at the time, but in fact it was the car of the immediate future and would have its influence on the external appearance of many British cars in the early 1950's. Many of its features indeed were desirable improvements: the all-round visibility, the good view of the road over the low bonnet, the low centre of gravity making for improved road-holding, the incorpora-tion of mudguards into the body shell giving smooth outline and better streamlining, and the large square luggage boot.

It was not until about five years after the end of the war that truly post-war designs began to emerge from the English factories. The new family saloons like the Standard Vanguard, the Ford Zephyr and the Vauxhall Velox provided standards of cruising speed, acceleration, driving visibility and passenger space that were unknown in the home market before the war except in luxury and near-luxury cars. It is true that their higher power-to-weight ratio,

144

Above: The neat Hillman "Estate" car, one of the many makes of this increasingly popular "countryman" body style. *Below:* The Morris Minor, like most other small cars today, handles better than many of the more costly cars of the 'thirties.

The increasing popularity of continental motoring is persuading more manufacturers to offer both saloon and convertible versions of the same model. Here are the two guises of the 1958 1½-litre Sunbeam Rapier. The modern convertible (with heater) is just as rain-proof, draught-proof and warm as the permanently closed saloon. It seems a pity that it has to be so much more expensive.

The 1959 Triumph "Herald", a striking example of
modern small-car designing.

combined with small road wheels, though giving fairly exciting performance on dry straight roads, made them dangerously prone to
slide on wet bends and to wheel spin when getting away uphill
from traffic lights, but in later models this trouble has been largely
cured by improved suspension and by lowering the true centre of
gravity.

At last the ending of Pool petrol and the availability of higher
octane premier-grade spirit made possible the marketing of the
higher compression engine. And thanks to the introduction of the
even higher octane Super grades in 1956, compression ratios in
perfectly ordinary family saloons are now commonly 8 to 1, or
higher – and will certainly rise higher still. This development,
coupled with subtle improvements in the design of combustion
chambers, valve ports, distributors and carburettors, has given a
new lease of life to the internal combustion piston engine, actually
increasing its output by over 50 per cent since 1939.

The biggest general change has been the shortening of stroke in
relation to bore, and there are now signs of a new trend towards

The Rover goes longer, lower and wider: the 1958 3-litre

larger, slower-running engines with a view to reducing wear and noise and giving greater flexibility in performance, yet with a negligible increase in fuel consumption. It would indeed seem that, except in the real economy class of car, customers are nowadays on the whole more inclined to be interested in performance than in squeezing that extra mile to the gallon (though you would hardly think so sometimes from the speed at which many motorists still seem content to meander along the narrow English main roads). Certainly this preference for fast performance as against fuel economy is true of the greater part of the export market, for in most countries motor spirit carries a smaller rate of tax than it does in Great Britain.

It can undoubtedly be said that the motor car has now emerged from the doldrums of the 'thirties and picked up its trade wind at last. From the point of view of both design and technical advance, we are living in a period of more rapid development than at any other time between 1919 and 1959. All drivers of modern cars, in whatever price range, enjoy standards of road-holding and passenger comfort that were dreamed of but rarely achieved between the

Both Citroën and Renault have assembly factories in England. *Above:* the Citroën ID.19, a simplified version of the famous DS.19. *Below:* the new Renault Floride, a striking advance on its sister Dauphine.

Still "the best car in the world". This Silver Wraith touring limousine has coachwork by H. J. Mulliner.

wars – or even ten years ago. So much so that the committee of the Vintage Sports Car Club have been able to declare that "since the war most of the faults we criticized so vociferously in the cars of the 'thirties have gradually been eradicated from modern design, and we no longer claim that our Vintage cars are 'better' than their modern equivalents in quality."

Overdrive, the automatic clutch, fully automatic transmission, power-assisted steering, disc brakes, independent suspension on all wheels, greater window-space for all-round visibility – all these and other means to greater safety are gradually becoming more available down the price scale. It will probably not be long before the clutch, the gear lever and the drum brake are thrown on the scrap-heap.

The march of science and design, however, in motoring as in other fields, creates new dangers and problems. Greater speed and acceleration obviously make the motor car an increasingly lethal weapon in the hands of the thoughtless or wanton, and swifter braking applied by an inexperienced driver can result in some pretty nasty skidding. The curved windscreen, which has contributed

Luxurious sports car. The Bentley "Continental" drop-head coupé by
Park Ward.

to road safety by improving the driver's forward visibility, has
ironically introduced a new motoring hazard – one which incidentally happened to the writer when he was doing about fifty. It is
an alarming experience. You are driving along quite peacefully,
anticipating the lunch you are going to enjoy when you reach your
destination – and suddenly a silent, white explosion blots out your
vision. Your windscreen, though still "intact", has splintered into
thousands of minute pebbles and become more opaque than frosted
glass. You push a bare fist through it and drive on to the next
garage, peering through the hole with reddening eyeballs.

Such incidents were at first thought to be caused by air pellets
fired by small boys concealed in the bushes, but they were more
probably due to a combination of tensions, several of which could
coincide at unlucky moments: the screen not fitting quite accurately
in its rubber mount; the difference in temperature between cold air
outside and heated air inside, making the outer surface of the curved
glass contract and the inner surface expand; a critical vibration set
up by the drumming of the tyres on certain road surfaces; and

The Italian influence in body-styling. The 1958 Standard Vanguard was restyled by Vignale, and recently the British Motor Corporation engaged Farina to design the bodies for many of their diverse range. Above are the 1959 Wolseley 15/60 and Austin A.55, bearing an unmistakable family resemblance to each other.

The Vauxhall Cresta, on the other hand, shows a strong transatlantic
influence.

perhaps a small flying stone kicked up by another car to administer
the *coup de grâce*. It is an experience not to be recommended at high
speed during the evening rush hour. It is strongly suspected that
this trouble may well have been the cause of many otherwise
inexplicable accidents to solitary drivers.

In recent years body-styling has become simpler, smoother and
sleeker in the constant effort to solve the basic body design problem –
that of finding a satisfactory compromise between the aerodynamic
streamlining of the racing car and the human requirements of
passenger comfort. Curves are subtler, projections are being smoothed
out, and there are even welcome signs that the fashion for excessive
chromium is at last beginning to die out.

Unfortunately the trend towards brighter colours has given new
scope and direction for further outbursts of questionable taste.
However, although certain two-tone juxtapositions are dangerously
distracting to the sensitive eye, it must be agreed that there is a
good deal to be said for brighter colours, especially on the grounds
of their contribution to safety. A recent letter in *The Times* put

Two B.M.A. sports cars deservedly popular in the U.S.A.—the M.G. "A." two-seater (*above*) and the Austin-Healey 100 Six.

forward the suggestion that many of the accidents and near-misses experienced by motorists could be avoided if cars and other vehicles were painted in bright colours to make them stand out from the background, especially during that often grey and shadowless quarter-of-an-hour before lighting-up time. Much research was done during the war by camouflage experts with the object of making ships, tanks, and other military targets less visible; their experience might be useful in achieving the opposite effect. Already much has been done to make civil aircraft more visible to each other in the sky.

The growth in British car exports since the war has been one of the important and encouraging factors in the recovery of British trade. During 1958 Britain produced over a million cars in the year for the first time – and nearly a half went to export markets. In the immediate post-war years, unfortunately, Britain made a some-what premature entry into the export markets. Admittedly the country's post-war economic difficulties called for desperate measures at the time, but it soon became clear that it was a short-sighted policy to attack dollar markets before the manufacturers were ready with true post-war designs and fully prepared sales and spare-parts organizations. The result was that British cars as a whole developed an undesirable reputation in this respect, a reputation which stuck for some time after the trouble had in fact been abundantly cured. The West German Volkswagen concern, by contrast, sensibly waited until they were ready with a supporting spare-part service before they launched their attack on the foreign markets. So although British manufacturers had despite all their difficulties captured over half the world car export market by 1950, seven years later their share, though larger in actual quantity owing to the rapidly ex-panding total, had dropped to less than 30 per cent. Meanwhile, the West Germans, starting from scratch, had quickly forged ahead to take 35 per cent (France's share in the same year being 15 per cent, America's 10 per cent, and Italy's 8 per cent).

Nevertheless, British manufacturers must be congratulated on their export achievements in the North American field. The steady increase in the size of the average American car – which has become so wide that it can be driven only with difficulty in many European city streets—is largely due to the high U.S.A. labour costs, which

Remarkable value for money. The smart Jaguar XK.150 drop-head and
the extremely successful Jaguar 2.4-litre saloon.

make it almost as expensive to make a small car as a large one. So much so that in recent years it became extremely difficult for America – birthplace of the Model T Ford! – to manufacture a really moderately priced motor. This situation left a gap in the American home market through which British and other European manufacturers were able to gain a surprisingly firm foothold in this traditionally "tough" export field.

The M.G. was quickly off the mark for Britain after the war – it had, incidentally, been one of the few British cars to win any sort of success in the U.S.A. before the war. It sparked off quite a sports-car craze and established a valuable quality-for-price reputation. Besides the M.G., the British Motor Corporation also sell Healey, Austin and Morris cars in satisfactory quantities in the U.S.A., netting altogether over a third of the total British sales there. Other strong teams from Britain are the Hillmans and Sunbeams of the Rootes Group, the Standard Triumph organization, Fords of Dagenham, and Jaguars (who suffered considerably from the fall in production

The A.C. 2-litre sports car makes its bow at the 1952 Motor Show

Graceful, subtle, powerful. The Bristol-engined A.C. "Ace" in coupé and sports car versions.

after their works fire at Coventry in 1957 but have since made an outstanding recovery). Most of these firms now have vigorous permanent organizations in the United States, making full use of the great American publicity machine to punch home the special qualities of their products. Rolls-Royce advertising has been surpassing the Americans at their own game with such talk-of-the-town slogans as "At 60 miles an hour the loudest noise in the Rolls-Royce is the ticking of the electric clock", and "People who feel diffident about driving a Rolls-Royce can buy a Bentley". (During 1958 the rate of Rolls-Royce sales in the U.S.A. went up by over 200 per cent.)

Although competing vigorously against each other, the British car importers in America join hands once a year in an imaginative piece of co-operative publicity, a mass demonstration of British cars on the Lime Rock racetrack in Connecticut. Here hundreds of American journalists and broadcasters are given the opportunity of trying out the new cars at speeds for themselves. This mass demonstration has been taking place annually since 1956 and has already become something of an institution.

It is true that the large size of the average American family makes a large car essential as the main family car, but the steady increase in the sales of the foreign, small car shows that more and more Americans are beginning to feel a revulsion against the inflated "space-machines" or "road-cruisers" which have for so long been their symbols of social progress. It has now in fact become smart to own a foreign car—if not as the main car, then as the second or third car. During 1958 nearly half a million British and other foreign cars were imported into the United States. During the first quarter of 1959 British cars alone sold to the tune of over 40,000 cars as compared with just over 22,000 in the corresponding quarter of 1958.

For several years European exporters have been batting well on this good wicket, and – except for the Nash "Rambler" and the Studebaker "Lark" – the big American manufacturers in Detroit showed little sign of being anxious to compete. Instead we have had the curious situation of (for instance) American Ford importing the English Ford and General Motors importing the English Vauxhall. Detroit was of course well aware of this growing market for the

Race meetings have become more popular than ever. *Above:* the start of a Production Car Race at Silverstone in 1950. *Below:* Coming into Woodcote Corner during the Nine Hours Race in 1955.

The crowds which attended the first R.A.C. Grand Prix since 1927, held at the newly opened course at Silverstone in 1948, astonished even the organizers. When Brooklands was abandoned immediately after the war the outlook had seemed black indeed, but its place has been more than adequately filled by Silverstone, Goodwood, Aintree and — for the smaller events – Brands Hatch, Oulton Park and others. Above is a view from the pits of the start of the 1958 British Grand Prix at Silverstone. In the front row: 7, Stirling Moss in a Vanwall; 20, Harry Schell in a B.R.M.; 10, Roy Salvadori in a Cooper-Climax. In the second row: 17, C. Allison in a Lotus-Climax; 1, Peter Collins in a Ferrari; 2, Mike Hawthorn in a Ferrari. The race was won by Peter Collins, with Mike Hawthorn second.

well-made small car, but so long as that market remained comparatively limited most American manufacturers were content to watch from the sidelines, waiting for the moment when the demand should grow to the point where they could produce a competitive article in really economic quantities. During 1959 this crucial moment arrived; several of the big firms announced plans for the production of what they prefer to call the "compact" or "personal" car (each one, needless to say, trying to make clear that *his* small car was going to be larger, roomier and wider than any other small car!).

So British and European exporters are finding themselves up against fiercer competition in the American small car field, not only in the United States but in other markets where in recent years the large American car had been losing ground.

There is no doubt that a major contribution to the success of British car exports has been the heart-warming return of British cars and drivers to the forefront of the racing world. Not since the Vintage years has the chequered flag been lowered so often for the green cars – and that applies to every form of car racing, Grand Prix, sports-car racing and international rallies.

Jaguars, the most successful of the sports cars now being exported from England, have revived – perhaps surpassed – memories of the Bentley victories at Le Mans. Jaguars won that gruelling twenty-four-hour contest in 1951, took first, second and fourth places in 1953, second place in 1954, and first place again in each of the three following years. Sir William Lyons then decided to withdraw for a while from official entry in competitive events in order to concentrate on putting the hard-won racing experience into his production cars.

Since the David Brown organization acquired Aston Martin Ltd in 1947 (and Lagonda Cars Ltd at the same time), the firm have pursued a vigorous racing policy and are now concentrating on Formula 1 after a successful debut at Silverstone. In 1959 Aston Martins won the World Sports Car Championship - the first time ever by a British firm. They at last succeeded in winning Le Mans outright, gaining both first and second places against strong Ferrari and Porsche opposition.

Above, the C-type Jaguar which won the 1953 Le Mans, exceeding an average of 100 m.p.h. for the first time in the history of the race. *Below:* a D-type Jaguar, similar to those which came first at Le Mans in 1956, 1957 and 1958.

The 3.7-litre Aston Martin DB 4 saloon introduced at the Paris Salon in 1958. The DB 4 is claimed to have the highest performance of any 4-seater production car. It can accelerate from 0–100 m.p.h. and stop again in just over 26 seconds.

It was a well-deserved victory, for in previous years they had come first in the 3-litre class four times and twice finished second overall. Their finest achievement, however, has been their triumph three years in succession in the Nürburgring 1,000 kilometres sports-car race, culminating in the 1959 event when Stirling Moss driving the only works-entered DBR 1/300, twice beat his own lap record of the previous year and twice regained the lead to snatch a thrilling victory from the strong Ferrari and Porsche teams.

Amongst the smaller specialist sports car manufacturers who have achieved success in competition Cooper and Lotus have been outstanding, but A.C., Frazer Nash, Allard, Austin-Healey, Triumph

Mr. G. A. Vandervell's Vanwall Specials brought new hope too for Britain
in Formula 1 racing when they made their first appearance in 1954, but it
was not until 1956 that, after many modifications, they began to win
important races. In 1958 they carried all before them. Above is one of the
Vanwalls, with Stirling Moss at the wheel.

and M.G., are all names to be conjured with in the current sports
car field.

In the purely racing field perhaps the most striking British con-
tender has been Mr Vandervell's Vanwall, which steadily developed
into a true world-beater. The great Vanwall year was 1958, when
these cars carried off the World Manufacturers' Championship by
winning six of the ten Formula 1 events in the face of strong foreign
opposition – though it must be remembered that the well-nigh
unbeatable Mercedes team of 1954 and 1955 was no longer in the
field, having temporarily withdrawn from racing. It was a sad day
for Britain when, at the end of his crowning year, ill-health com-
pelled Mr. Vandervell to announce the withdrawal of the Vanwall,
too, from racing – but not, as it turned out, for long.

Ever since its first appearance at Silverstone in 1950 the white
hope of British racing has been the B.R.M., designed by Peter

From high hope through disappointment to success. The B.R.M., seen above,
at its first showing to the Press, closely guarded by two policemen as British
as the car itself, consistently failed to live up to expectations, but a later
horse from this stable at last won its first *grande épreuve* with Bonnier's victory
in the 1959 Grand Prix of Holland at Zandvoort.

Berthon. The initials stand for British Racing Motors, the concern
which was formed after the war under Raymond Mays' inspiration
to develop a car that would regain Britain's prestige in international
Grand Prix racing. Unfortunately the B.R.M., now sponsored by
the enthusiastic industrialist Mr A. G. B. Owen, has suffered more
than the normal quota of teething troubles, partly owing to the
originality of its design; despite a fair crop of minor successes its
career had until recently been one long series of heartbreaking
disappointments. At last, however, a B.R.M. victory was achieved in
the 1959 Grand Prix of Holland in the hands of Joakim Bonnier of
Sweden, and everyone with British motor racing at heart must hope
that a new and more rewarding future has now opened up for this
potentially outstanding racing machine.

The remarkably rapid rise of Cooper cars to a leading position
in international sports car and formula racing has been a prominent

feature of recent competitive motoring. Their Formula 2 car not only won the 1958 manufacturers' World Championship in its class but came third to Vanwall and Ferrari overall. Stirling Moss won the 1958 Grand Prix of Argentina in a 1960 c.c. Cooper. During 1959, with a works team consisting of Jack Brabham, Masten Gregory and Bruce McLaren, Cooper cars have been in the forefront of Formula 1 racing.

For the commercial sports car and the high-performance "ordinary" car the Rally is as invaluable a proving ground as ever, and in recent years this form of competition has been attracting more interest and participation than ever before. Jaguars, M.G.s, Aston Martins, Fords, Sunbeams and others are regularly entered every year for such weakness-probing tests as the Monte Carlo Rally, the Alpine Rally, the Tulip Rally and – on home ground – the R.A.C. Rally, partly for the publicity gained by success and partly for the experience gained by failure.

Sidney Allard (*left*) and his co-drivers Guy Warburton and Tom Lush with the Allard Special in which they won the Monte Carlo Rally of 1952. In the same year an Allard took third place at Le Mans.

Italy's Ferraris have been one of the most formidable teams in post-war Formula 1 racing. Here is the late Peter Collins driving the winning Ferrari in the British Grand Prix at Silverstone in July 1958.

All forms of motor sport are now attracting more public support than they did before the war. This has in turn encouraged more manufacterers to participate, and as a result there is available on the market today a greater variety of well-tried and excellent sports cars than at any other time in history.

It is truer than ever that racing improves the breed. The fierceness of competition in the export markets ensures that the production car gets the earliest possible benefit from the improvements in design and material made – to all standard components as well as to engines and bodies – as the direct result of racing experience.

It is not only the individual manufacturers of production cars who have seen their export sales benefit from their own achievements in road and track events. British cars as a whole have gained immeasurably in prestige from the really remarkable demonstrations of British engineering excellence and driving skill which the last few years have seen.

The worst crash in motor racing history occurred shortly after the start of the 1955 Le Mans 24-hour Endurance Race. The picture above shows the moment immediately after Pierre Levegh's Mercedes-Benz touched the tail of Lance Macklin's Austin-Healey (just visible in the foreground), spun, somersaulted, hit the barrier and exploded into the packed spectators, killing over 80 people and seriously injuring some 100 others. The race continued, and was won by Hawthorn in a Jaguar.

Facing, above: Jockeying for position in the early stages of the 1957 Monza Grand Prix of Italy. Although lying last in this picture, Stirling Moss in his Vanwall (No. 18) went on to win. The leading car (No. 2) is Fangio's Maserati. Nos. 22 and 20 are Vanwalls.

Facing, below: Colin Chapman has played an influential part in recent design developments. He was responsible for important modifications in the B.R.M., designed the chassis for the Vanwall, and has been making Lotus cars since 1952. Lotus and Cooper cars now pretty well dominate the sports-car events in this country. Four basic types of Lotus sports cars are marketed: the sports-racing Mark 11 and Mark 15, the fast touring Élite coupé (shown here), all with Coventry-Climax engines, and the "Seven" with a Ford 1172 c.c. engine.

168

Cooper success. *Above:* The Formula 2 model which won the 1958 manufacturers' World Championship in its class. *Below:* The new Formula 1
car, announced in 1959, powered by a 2½-litre Coventry Climax engine.

The 1950's have been notable for the steady rise of British drivers to a well-nigh dominating position in international racing. By the middle of the decade most of the leading British drivers, including Reg Parnell, Ken Wharton, Lance Macklin, Stirling Moss, Mike Hawthorn, Peter Collins, were being regularly employed by foreign *équipes*. *Above:* Peter Collins and Mike Hawthorn are seen together after taking first and second places respectively in the 1958 British Grand Prix at Silverstone—both driving Ferraris (this was one of the big races that Vanwall did *not* win that year, failing to repeat their splendid victory in the same event the previous year). Within a short space of time both these young and successful drivers were dead—Collins being killed in the German Grand Prix at Nürburgring a few weeks later, and Hawthorn (World Champion Driver of 1958) in a road crash at Guildford in the following January.

171

The greatest racing driver of the early 1950's, the Argentinian Juan Manuel Fangio. Driving at various times for Alfa-Romeo, Maserati, Ferrari and Mercedes, he had been World Champion several times running. He retired at the end of the 1958 season.

Tony Brooks began racing in 1952. Until 1959 he drove only British cars—Connaughts, Vanwalls and Aston Martins—but in that year he became Ferrari's No. 1 driver. Given equal mounts, Brooks is perhaps the only other British driver who can seriously challenge Moss.

Stirling Moss, undoubtedly Britain's most brilliant racing driver today. Perhaps his finest wins have been the 1955 Mille Miglia in a Mercedes, the 1957 Grand Prix d'Europe in a Vanwall, the 1958 Argentine Grand Prix in a Cooper, and the 1959 Nürburgring 1,000 kilometres sports car race in an Aston Martin. More than his fair share of mechanical failures has so far robbed him of the world championship.

Jack Brabham, the Australian member of the Cooper works team. Although very experienced on Australian circuits, he did not come to England until 1955 and only began driving in Formula 1 competition in 1957. He won the Formula 2 world championship of 1958. After his victories at Monaco and in the British Grand Prix he was well in the running for the Formula 1 world championship of 1959.

CHAPTER 13

Mr Mercury Going Places

Meanwhile, how had National Benzole been faring? At the end of the war the head office staff had reluctantly abandoned the rural seclusion of Stonor Park and returned to the hurly-burly of Wellington House to gird their loins for the eventual renewal of competition. In many ways it was a frustrating time, for though the Petroleum Board was disbanded (or, to use the hideous word coined in the trade, "demerged") in 1948, political considerations delayed the return to branded spirits until 1953, over seven years after the end of hostilities.

Until the Pool was allowed to run dry, therefore, the motor spirit companies had to content themselves with preparing the ground, reminding the public of their separate entities and wooing a new generation of motorists for their future custom. National Benzole entertainingly developed the theme of "Motor how you will . . . Mr Mercury will give you more miles per gallon," accompanied by amusing drawings of unlikely looking motorists driving even more unlikely looking vehicles. Here was an elephant lapping the circus ring on a motorized pedestal; here a plump Cockney couple speeding to the Derby on a carriage that was indeed, but only just, horseless; here a city man leaving home in the morning in his one-cylinder, chain-driven garage on wheels – and at the foot of the advertisements the familiar head of Mr Mercury waiting behind a National Benzole Mixture pump.

In 1941 Mr Henshaw retired from the office of Chairman. After the Petroleum Board days—in 1949—his place was taken by Mr Hittinger, who through his successive posts as Secretary (1920), General Manager (1925), Managing Director (1938) and Deputy Chairman (1941) had done so much to steer the pirate ship for thirty years. As a team they had brought it safely through the shoal waters.

In January 1951 the Company's research department, whose Willesden laboratories had been destroyed in the war, moved into newly equipped laboratories alongside the Watford by-pass. Here, under the direction of the Company's Chief Chemist, Mr G. Claxton (his former colleague and co-author W. Hoffert having died in 1949) work continued on research and analysis control for the Company and for the benzole industry. All the products of the country's 74 benzole refineries, and the Company's 300 different grades of lubricating oils, industrial oils, greases and anti-freeze compounds were constantly tested and analysed to ensure that they were up to specification.

At last, on February 1st, 1953, the motor fuel companies were allowed, for the first time for over thirteen years, to market their spirits under their own branded names. The fight was on again, and it became clear at once that the pace of competition was going to be fiercer than ever. National Benzole's advertising returned to the attack with all its old verve, still playing new variations on what has, after all, been the same basic "selling story" ever since the earliest days. This time the approach was fresh and boldly technical: an attempt, highly successful in the upshot, to make the still increasing motoring public "aromatics" conscious, to explain what the aromatic hydro-carbons were and why National Benzole Mixture's high-aromatic content made it more powerful and "knock"-resistant than any other motor spirit. This theme developed later into the "Wow, Aromatics!" campaign which, though held by some motoring purists to encourage an undesirably reckless attitude towards fast driving, did illustrate most effectively the sense of exhilaration experienced by motorists trying the Mixture for the first time.

Improvements in petroleum refining techniques since the war, and the development of higher-octane fuels, had opened the way for car manufacturers to produce higher-compression engines. In 1953 the new premier grade spirits were of higher quality than their

175

pre-war namesakes. Then in 1956 motor spirits in the 100-octane range made their appearance to meet the needs of the new engines. Amongst the first of these was Super National Benzole, which is a powerful blend of benzole and high-octane petrol.

The ramifications of the uses of benzole in modern industry would have seemed unbelievable forty years ago. The chemical industry alone absorbs nearly forty million gallons a year. Benzole is needed, for instance, in ever-increasing quantities in the production of aniline dyes, which not only provide a range of over five thousand different colours for domestic use but also aid medical research in the dyeing of bacteria to make them more conspicuous under the microscope. It is an essential ingredient in the manufacture of D.D.T. and other insecticides which have revolutionized the work of farmers and gardeners in the short space of seventeen years (it seems incredible that D.D.T. only came into general use in 1942). The modern synthetic perfumes would not exist if it were not for the benzole on which they are based; the perfume of flowers was for centuries distilled from the oil in the flowers themselves, and as several tons of flowers were needed to produce one ounce of the oil it will be readily understood that the "aromatics" in benzole have made an important contribution to the comparative cheapness of modern perfumes.

Benzole also helps to make nylon – a gallon is enough for about 150 pairs of stockings – but not all nylon ends up as .0035-inch diameter thread for stockings; industry uses it for certain types of gear wheels, cams, bearings, valve seats, brushes, and as a substitute for "gut" for fishing tackle, surgical stitches and so on. Polystyrene, another important plastic made from benzole, has a thousand uses from toothbrushes to car facia panels. Benzole is also an invaluable ingredient in modern solvents and detergents.

The use of benzole in the making of explosives has already been mentioned, but it is fair to say that by its contribution to the manufacture of drugs it has helped to save and prolong millions more lives than it has destroyed in the brutality of war. In the course of his pioneer work on antiseptics, Lister was the first to make medicinal use of phenol, or carbolic acid, a benzole derivative. Ever since the German dyestuffs industry in the early years of this century first

Thrashing along through the Straits of Dover goes the motor vessel *Ben
Hittinger*, one of the "Ben Boat" fleet of coastal tankers built up over the
years by the National Benzole Company, all named after its Directors. The
Marine Department came into operation within four years of the Company's
inauguration. Its part in the Second World War is recounted in the text
of this book.

appreciated the biochemical action of certain of the aniline dyes, benzole has played an increasing role in the development of healing and antiseptic drugs: pain-killers like aspirin; phenobarbitone and other sedatives; acriflavin, gentian violet and other germicides; the range of sulphanilamide drugs like M & B 693 which saved so many lives during the last war; salvarsan, which enables living organisms within the human body to be killed without harm to the body itself and so made possible the cure of parasitic diseases like syphilis, sleeping sickness and malaria; dicoumarin, whose ability to prevent the formation of blood clots makes it a valuable aid in the treatment of thrombosis. Most important of all, perhaps, is the successful treatment of cancer of the prostate gland by a benzole-based synthetic hormone, which represents chemotherapy's only positive victory so far in the fight against cancer.

Since the last war, then, the industrial and chemical uses of benzole have multiplied to an extraordinary extent, and the benzole marketing scene has undergone a subtle but profound change. So much so that the situation of 1919, when the gas and steel industries looked to the National Benzole Company to "unload" the surplus by-product of the coking ovens, no longer obtains today. Moreover, since the war the marketing of motor spirit has become highly specialized and competitive. The companies have been tending towards exclusive long-term agreements with selected garages and filling stations, entailing a much closer interest in retail marketing and the investment of more capital in the distributing side of the business.

All these factors contributed towards far-reaching decisions taken by the benzole producers and put into effect in 1957. A new company, Benzole Producers Ltd, was formed to cope with the increasing volume and complexity of the industrial benzole market. At the same time it seemed appropriate to the producers to withdraw from direct interest in the motor spirit and other petroleum business of the National Benzole Company. Negotiations were opened up with Shell-Mex and B.P. Ltd, who have for many years supplied the petrol for the benzole mixtures, and the ownership of the marketing company passed to them. The result was a re-birth of the National Benzole Company as a vigorous marketing organization, able to

concentrate on the sale of its goods in this highly competitive period. More than that, Mr Mercury has been able to spread his wings over new fields in the vast new petroleum product market.

The year 1957, therefore, marked the beginning of a new phase in the Company's history – and provides a climax to this account of its first forty years that would no doubt have seemed beyond the bounds of credibility to those early pirates of the Horseferry Road.

In the early months of 1959 the London headquarters moved from Wellington House to Mercury House, one of the magnificent new modern buildings which are transforming the Knightsbridge skyline. The National Benzole Company have certainly come a long way since 1919, and it seems that Mr Mercury's winged feet are speeding towards the horizon as swiftly as ever.

The old and the new. Mr. Mercury himself has been given a face-lift to mark the Company's fortieth anniversary.

CHAPTER 14

The Future of Motoring

The first forty years of the National Benzole Company's history have certainly seen tremendous changes in the motoring scene. While the research chemists have been improving the quality and the power-potential of motor spirit, engineers and designers have learnt – through the complicated process of trial and error and under the spur of commercial and racing competition – how the internal combustion engine can use that spirit to greater advantage. Engines have become smaller and relatively more powerful.

What does the future hold? Many of the features of present-day cars will be past history by the end of this century. The clutch, the gear-lever and the drum brake are already on the way out. The carburettor may soon be ousted by increasing use of direct fuel injection into the cylinder, which can give better mixture control and greater fuel economy. And reports of new inventions are crowding in on us at an unprecedented rate.

Even the wheel – that most significant of Man's early inventions – appears to be in question. The British firm of Saunders-Roe and certain American manufacturers have already given practical demonstrations of the hovercraft principle, riding on air over water and land. It is difficult to see how this would work in a built-up area, for the air billowing out from underneath the craft would be a serious inconvenience to pedestrians. It might be possible, however, to make a car that runs on normal wheels in towns and on minor roads but switches over to "airborne" on reaching a motorway. Greater riding comfort on *all* roads is more likely to be achieved by a more general use of the pneumatic suspension system pioneered in recent years by Citroën.

What about the piston engine itself?

It is well known that Rovers have been experimenting with a gas-turbine car for some years. However, one of the disadvantages of the gas-turbine engine is the difficulty of making it efficient in a size small enough to be useful in the ordinary production car. The designers probably still have to get rid of the time-lag in response to the throttle, both in acceleration and deceleration. Even when these snags have been ironed out there remains the problem of how to put the gas-turbine engine on to an economic, mass-production basis. The stresses involved demand tougher and more expensive metals, and the degree of finish required is very high. Further developments on the gas-turbine car are therefore awaited with interest.

If nuclear energy holds any promise at all of application to road vehicle propulsion, it is unlikely to be in the form of self-contained power units. Although nuclear power units are already in actual use in certain kinds of ships, it seems improbable that they can ever be made small enough and light enough for use in road vehicles. If, however, someone could devise an electricity storage battery very much lighter and smaller than those available today, we might soon see a return to the electric car, with motorists dropping in at the filling station to exchange their run-down batteries for others ready charged from the nuclear-supplied national grid.

Another interesting idea, still in the research stage, is the possibility of "fuel cells" which could be topped up with petroleum fuel at the filling station and which could directly generate current capable of driving an electric motor.

But in this overcrowded island the problem for the more immediate future is the preservation of mobility. The high cruising speeds of which nearly all production cars are now capable are rarely used on the roads of Britain. There are something over eight million vehicles on those roads, and the number is increasing at the rate of half a million a year.

Although the surfacing of our minor roads makes them superior to those of most other countries, our narrow, tortuous and bottle-

The car of the future? Although conventional in appearance, this experimental Rover shown at the 1956 Motor Show housed the Rover T-3 turbine engine, less than half the size of the JET-1 engine which had achieved a speed of over 150 m.p.h. in trials in Belgium four years earlier. The rear-mounted engine drives all four wheels, and has no clutch and no gears.

necked major roads have been the laughing-stock of foreign tourists and the despair of all motorists. Happily the neglect of many years shows signs of coming to an end. Some of the money which motorists have been paying out in vehicle taxation is at last being ploughed back in the active construction of new motorways and by-passes and in the widening and straightening of existing main roads.

But equally urgent is the planning of more urban motorways to provide fast links between the centres of large towns and the main highways. One solution to this difficult problem would seem to lie in building overhead roads on stilts above existing railway tracks, which after all offer ready-made channels through heavily built-up areas. In big towns, where the morning and evening commuters' rush is a major problem, some of these overhead lanes could be made one-way light-traffic routes – inward only in the morning and outward only in the afternoon and evening, leaving traffic moving in the opposite direction to use the existing normal routes.

A more imaginative attack on the parking problem in large towns seems even more urgently necessary. At present, harassed authority, rightly concerned to keep traffic moving, is obliged to treat the parking motorist as a sort of petty criminal. But for better or worse motoring has become an integral part of modern civilization, and the motorist *ought* to be able to park his car conveniently without running the risk of a summons for obstruction. What is wanted is surely: an extension of the parking meter system, to provide for the motorist who has to move about and make frequent calls during the day; more experiment with other methods of street parking and off-street parking; and the construction of more multi-storey parking garages in which access to the various floors is either by means of a ramp, such as at Selfridges in London, or mechanically by lift, one of which has been built in Birmingham.

The road improvements now being planned and carried out will of course make a great contribution to road safety by eliminating many of the causes of accidents. Manufacturers, too, are constantly introducing new features to make their cars safer to handle in traffic and in bad road conditions and to reduce the seriousness of injuries in case of accident. Many of these desirable features are still "optional extras", but their widespread adoption would make a real contribution to safety. Wing mirrors, for instance, heaters for demisting and defrosting, screen washers for dirty weather – all essential aids to good visibility; fold-down arm-rests in the centre of front bench seats, to prevent drivers from being thrown off the steering-wheel in an emergency right-hand turn; collapsible, telescopic steering-columns and rubber-cushioned facia panels to reduce the injurious effect of collisions . . . and so on.

The widespread development of motorways will in itself create a new safety problem – the somnolence induced by the monotony of driving at high speed along a wide straight road. It has been suggested that the answer to this might be a sort of "automatic pilot" system whereby each car moves along over a leader cable which electrically maintains it on a steady course, the engine meanwhile kept to a steady speed by a governor and prevented from too close an approach to the car ahead by a radar warning device. It is doubtful, however, whether the prudent driver would be willing to place such implicit trust in a system of this kind.

The faster cars become, and the more there are of them on the road, the more important becomes the need to reduce accident causes. Unfortunately no amount of road improvement or mechanical safety aid can cater for the bad manners of some motorists and the stupidity or lack of skill of certain others. Severer penalties, including greater use of disqualification, seem to be called for as a deterrent against the wilfully dangerous driver. More difficult to cope with are the impatient gamblers who overtake on blind corners or jump the queue on the assumption that others will "let them in" when they have to get out of the way of approaching trouble – and the drivers who never have accidents themselves but often create conditions which encourage accidents to others. Finally there are the accident-prone – those who, though rarely legally in the wrong, are frequently involved in some mishap or other, possibly due to forgetting the useful axiom that there is always likely to be a fool round the next corner. Stiffer initial driving tests, possibly repeated at, say, five-year intervals, might eliminate some of the more incompetent drivers.

One way and another, there is no doubt that we are in a period of exciting and rapid development. Although the spark ignition petrol engine is capable of further development it may quite soon be meeting serious competition in passenger cars from developments of the Diesel and the gas turbine. However, it seems unlikely to be supplanted as the power unit for the ordinary car for many years and it will continue to be well served by the aromatic hydrocarbons which benzole contains in so generous a measure.

A Great British Industry

For some time after the war the increasing use of benzole as a raw material in so many modern industries raised the demand to a point where it exceeded the supply. But in recent years tremendous progress has been made in the modernization of gas undertakings and the creation of new coke ovens – the new National Coal Board coking plant and benzole refinery at Nantgarw, South Wales, and the new plant at Chesterfield, the vast new Steel Company of Wales, the new plants of Dorman Long at Middlesbrough, of Colville's at Tolcross near Glasgow, of John Summers & Co. at Shotton, Flint-shire – these, and others still in the planning stage, are adding millions of gallons a year to the total output.

Benzole starts in the vast fossilized coal deposits under the soil of Britain. From the mines the raw coal is delivered to the great coking oven plants, the gas-works and the iron and steel works, where the coal is baked at colossal temperatures. Gas is given off, and the residue of coke goes off to feed blast furnaces and domestic boilers. The gas is drawn away and subjected to a series of separating processes, the first by-product to be removed being tar, used in road-building and a wide range of chemical products. The gas then bubbles up through water, leaving behind its ammonia content to be used in the production of sulphate of ammonia for fertilizers and so on, and passes on to the giant scrubbing-towers whose tall columns are such a characteristic feature of the modern coking plant. The gas enters at the bottom of the tower and ascends through a falling spray of wash-oil which absorbs the benzole. From the top of the tower the gas is led through a purifier and thence to gas-holders for storage and eventual piping to the domestic customer. From the bottom of the tower the absorption oil flows away through a heat-exchanger to the still where it percolates downwards through high-pressure steam. The steam vaporizes the benzole and draws it off in gaseous form. The oil drops down and returns to the scrubbing tower to do its job all over again, while the gaseous mixture of benzole and steam goes through a condenser to be separated; the benzole floats on the water and can then be drawn off separately into storage tanks. At the refineries the crude benzole is washed first with sulphuric acid to remove impurities, then with water and soda to neutralize the acid, and finally with water again to remove the last traces of the refining agents. Washing completed, the benzole goes into a "rectification" still for one final distillation before emerging as a crystal clear liquid ready to be blended with petrol and transported to storage depots by rail, road and sea.

From every ton of coal approximately 3 gallons of benzole can be recovered. If the benzole were not recovered in the coke ovens the cost of gas and coke would be considerably higher than they are (coke would be about 7s. a ton dearer), and Britain would have to find dollars or other foreign currency to buy millions more gallons of oil from overseas than she does at present.

But coal is still used for the most part as a raw fuel, in domestic fires, factories, railway engines and so on. Over ten per cent of this goes up in smoke, polluting the air of cities and eating into the stone-work of buildings. It has been estimated that over six million tons of coal a year vanish unused in this way – and quite a slice of that tonnage consists of the valuable aromatic hydrocarbons which go to make up benzole.

This matter of "aromatics" is not just an advertising "gimmick". The hydrocarbons of which motor spirit is composed are divided by the chemists into groups, such as naphthenes, paraffins, olefines, and so on. The aromatic group (so-called, as we saw in an earlier chapter, because of their age-old derivation from sweet-smelling spices) have long been recognized as having a greater resistance to engine "knock" than any other group. All motor spirits contain aromatics to a certain degree, and considerable effort is spent in modern refineries on "cracking" and reforming to turn some of the less useful hydrocarbons into aromatics. Benzole, which consists almost entirely of aromatics, contains a higher proportion of carbon to hydrogen than other motor spirit. The formula, for those who understand these things, consists of six atoms of carbon combined with six of hydrogen, in the form of a ring so constructed that the possibilities of interchanging and rearranging them to combine with other substances are almost without limit. This chemical composition has the virtue of enabling benzole to burn more smoothly in the cylinder, thus avoiding "knock". But the great advantage of benzole over tetraethyl lead and other anti-knock "additives" is that it is a fuel in itself. Being heavier than petrol it also has a higher calorific value. In other words, a gallon of benzole weighs more and gives more energy than a gallon of petrol.

When benzole first came into use as a motor fuel it was merely as an alternative to petrol and not because it was considered to have any special advantages. On the contrary, it seemed at first to have certain disadvantages. Its higher carbon-hydrogen ratio gave rise to excessive carbon deposit in the engine; it was also thought that its higher calorific value would lead to over-heating. Its anti-knock value was not only unrecognized but of little importance because at that time the compression ratios of engines were so much lower.

The theoretical disadvantages, of course, though emphasized by benzole's competitors, did not materialize in fact. Excessive carbon was avoided by a slight adjustment to the carburettor, and even this became unnecessary with a benzole-petrol mixture. There was no over-heating but rather an increase in the power obtained per gallon. And when, of course, the compression ratios of engines began to rise benzole's anti-knock properties came into their own.

It remains true today that, in the words of the old National Benzole Mixture slogan, "benzole makes good petrol better". One might extend this to say that benzole makes Super petrol better still.

The future of benzole, like that of all fuels, is full of unknown problems. It is estimated that the world demand for liquid fuels will *double* itself during the next ten years. How soon the development of nuclear energy will make itself felt on a significant scale it is not easy to guess; much depends on its ability to provide cheap mobile power through other media besides the electricity grid. But it certainly looks as though benzole will be wanted in the motoring world for many years yet, and to its industrial and chemical uses there seems no end.

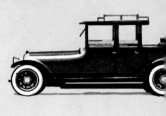